F

# Money Doesn't Grow on Trees

## A PARENT'S GUIDE
## TO RAISING
## FINANCIALLY RESPONSIBLE CHILDREN

*Neale S. Godfrey*
*and Carolina Edwards*

A Fireside Book
Published by Simon & Schuster

New York  London  Toronto  Sydney  Tokyo  Singapore

FIRESIDE
Rockefeller Center
1230 Avenue of the Americas
New York, New York 10020

FIRESIDE and colophon are registered trademarks
of Simon & Schuster Inc.

DESIGNED BY BARBARA MARKS

Manufactured in the United States of America

1   3   5   7   9   10   8   6   4   2

Library of Congress Cataloging-in-Publication Data
Godfrey, Neale S.
Money doesn't grow on trees : a parent's guide to
raising financially responsible children /
Neale S. Godfrey and Carolina Edwards.
        p.      cm.
"A Fireside book."
Includes index.
1. Children—Finance, Personal.
2. Children's allowances.
3. Safety and thrift. I. Edwards, Carolina. II. Title.
        HG179.G63        1994
    649'.1—dc20                  93-36198    CIP
        ISBN 0-671-79805-7

# Acknowledgments

This book is a guidebook, and it is most appropriate to acknowledge all of the people who have helped to guide me through this process and, frankly, through my life.

It is only fitting to start with my mother, Georgine. She frequently reminds me that if she hadn't potty-trained me at the appropriate age, none of this would have happened. I formally acknowledge her for her guidance.

Thanks to my stepfather, Herb, who calls me his daughter and means it.

I want to thank my children, Kyle and Rhett, not only for being the super kids they are, but also for being my "guinea pigs." They are a living testimony to the fact that kids *can* grow up to be financially responsible.

My agent, Peter Ginsberg, not only listened,

but bought into the vision that we had to combat "financial illiteracy" now. He introduced me to Sydny Miner. Sydny's professional approach has made what could be a grueling process of publishing a book a dream.

Next, I want to thank Ralph. He has always been there to love me, and it is he with whom I have chosen to spend the rest of my life. Ralph rekindles my dream every time the flame flickers out and even throws logs on the fire to challenge and feed the blaze.

I'd also like to acknowledge my sisters, Malla and Alison. Their support and unconditional love have never waned. Thank you.

A special acknowledgment goes to my brother-in-law, Dr. Irving Dardik, the brightest and the most courageous man I know. I can only say that I love him like the brother I never had and thank him for showing me what real perseverance and talent are.

I want to close with warmest thanks to two of my special supporters and friends, George and Eric. They open doors that seem to be not only shut but bolted and padlocked. George is confident that we're going to get there and Eric keeps me from straying too far from the path.

—N.S.G.

N eale and I would like to thank several people who helped us with this book. We appreciate the professional generosity of two friends, psychiatrist Magda Polenz, M.D., and child psychiatrist Lenore Terr, M.D. Both women are the mothers of extremely successful children, and their input was invaluable. Wilhelm Morales was, as always, very gracious in allowing us to test many of the children's games in this book at Willie's Grocery. Anne Smith and Jeff Edwards were more than patient in clarifying certain legal and employee benefit policies, Judy Twersky and Andrea King added their creative thoughts, and many friends, but particularly Frank Viverito, Elaine Erenstein, and Debbie Harmison Byrne, relayed their experiences with their own children that greatly added to our body of knowledge.

—C.E.

*This book is dedicated to my best friend. She is the person who is always there: to accept my collect phone calls; to read me only my good horoscopes; to supply all of her friends with autographed copies of my book; to tell me not to lose any more weight when I'm struggling with my lifelong diet; to tell me I was brilliant on TV even when I know I couldn't find the camera with the light on; to give Ralph and me her blessing for our costume Halloween wedding when I know she's waiting for me to come to my senses; to love Ralph, my new husband, as much as I do; to give her financial tips to our radio audience; and especially to let our family celebrate the wonderful ninety-three years she's lived on this earth.*
*Granny Jewel, thank you.*

—N.S.G.

*To my beloved parents,*
*Bob and Virginia Edwards,*
*who gave me the kind of security in life*
*that money can't buy.*

—C.E.

# Contents

# Introduction: Why Your Children Must Be Fluent in Finance

*E*ver since Dr. Benjamin Spock's *What Every Baby Knows* hit the bestseller chart in 1954, anxious parents have devoured how-to books on raising disciplined, unneurotic children. Despite Dr. Spock's vision, however, and the hundreds of other literary contributions since, the task of child-rearing in the 1990s is more challenging, not less, than in the days of Donna Reed and TV dinners. Directional, or how-to, books on parenting are sought by a hungry, near-desperate audience who recognize that raising children is not a hobby but a life-long career.

While the body of literature on parenting deals with a range of subjects, it is odd that no book addresses one particularly vital skill that a child will use every day of his or her adult life: money management. The reason? The overwhelming majority of Americans—some say as high as 80 percent—don't understand finance themselves. How money works and, more important, how it can work for the person using it is a mystery to many, many otherwise intelligent people.

Experts say the result of this widespread "financial illiteracy" is evident on two levels—rising personal bankruptcy and a nearly incomprehensible national debt. It might be said that our personal torment over money exactly parallels the national financial disaster.

Why are our children headed for, or already well entrenched in, financial illiteracy? There are two compelling reasons. First, we as parents have not taught them. After all, who ever bothered to teach us anything about money?

Second, money is an emotionally charged subject. It is viewed as "the root of all evil," as a tool for power, or as a weapon to control others. Money evokes such strong emotions that it is cited as the number one reason for divorce in this country.

However, despite the fears or reluctance to discuss money that we may feel as adults, we cannot continue to pass this attitude on to yet another generation of consumers. Money is no more evil than electricity. Both have the ability to bring great security and comfort, or to inflict enormous distress and destruction. It is the user who decides.

Clearly the answer lies, at least in part, in education. Plenty is written, broadcast, and discussed about finance that is targeted to the adult consumer; very little is available for the younger, upcoming generation of consumers who will want to purchase cars, obtain mortgages, care for their aging parents, and hope to have the financial security that will enable them to lead independent, productive lives.

Couples, or the single parent, will find that children can be taught simple principles of money management at a surprisingly young age. In fact, many parents inadvertently give their toddlers a lesson in "money recognition" (the first step in learning about money management) every time they take coins out of their curious toddler's mouth.

The process of teaching money management does not have to be tedious. In fact, it can't be if a parent hopes to hold his child's attention for more than thirty seconds. The mandate for _Money Doesn't Grow on Trees_ is that learning be fun for the child and easy for the parent. The education starts with simple money recognition games and proceeds with on-site exercises at the grocery story, the bank, or anywhere money changes hands.

We called this book _Money Doesn't Grow on Trees_ because almost every parent in America has uttered this statement in frustration over his child's financial naivete. No, money doesn't grow on trees, but, with help, _it can grow!_

This book is designed to help a parent explain the basics of money management to children aged three through college. It deals with such intimidating financial terms as "debit" and "mortgage" as well as how to open a checking account or purchase stock. It offers instruction on allowance, budgeting, and even charitable giving. Most of all, _Money Doesn't Grow on Trees_ enables parents to give their children a gift that cannot be bought at any price: self-reliance.

—Neale S. Godfrey and Carolina Edwards

Editor's note: In order to eliminate the awkwardness of saying "he or she," we've alternated using male and female pronouns, and sometimes use the plural form.

Also, whenever possible, we've directed our instructions to specific age groups so that you can apply the information at your child's level.

# 1

## What Kind of (Financial) Personality Do You and Your Children Have?

All through history and saturating our literature are references to the greed and generosity of human beings. The name Scrooge has become synonymous with "tightwad"; Carnegie has come to represent cultural generosity. Who knows or remembers what Mr. Rockefeller did except give lots and lots of money to charity. Archie Bunker, on the other hand, was known to shut the blinds and turn out all the lights on Halloween to avoid giving out free candy to children.

The truth is that money affects us. No matter how much we have or don't have, it affects our mood, our marriage, our goals, our dreams, and our personalities.

In America, our great land of opportunity, the 1980s proved to be the decade of the spender. The indication thus far is that the 1990s will be governed by the savers. (We'll see who's left standing at the turn of the century, won't we?)

You are one of these, and the saving or spending part of your personality influences your child. Do you know if you are a spender or a saver? The following is a fourteen-question quiz to determine which financial personality type you are:

## THE ADULT FINANCIAL PERSONALITY TYPE QUIZ

1. Do you find yourself thinking about money often?
   Yes _____     No _____
2. Do you love watching your bank account grow?
   Yes _____     No _____
3. If you inherited a great deal of money today, would you save the bulk of it?
   Yes _____     No _____
4. Do you use your credit cards to the limit?
   Yes _____     No _____
5. Are you perpetually in debt at the end of each month?
   Yes _____     No _____
6. Do you feel it's important to buy the "right" things?
   Yes _____     No _____
7. Do you feel inferior to your friends financially?
   Yes _____     No _____
8. Does money give you a feeling of power?
   Yes _____     No _____
9. Are you afraid you'll run out of money and be left poor in your old age?
   Yes _____     No _____
10. Do you have a hard time making decisions about spending money, even if it's a small purchase?
    Yes _____     No _____
11. When your spouse says it's time to buy something, are the first words out of your mouth "We can't afford it"?
    Yes _____     No _____

12. If someone asked you, "How much money do you have in your purse or wallet?" would you know exactly?
Yes _____     No _____
13. Do you use shopping as a reward for yourself?
Yes _____     No _____
14. If it was a bad day, do you often buy yourself something to feel better?
Yes _____     No _____

How to Score: Yes answers to questions 1, 2, 3, 8, 9, 10, 11, and 12 indicate you are a saver. A yes answer to questions 4, 5, 6, 7, 13, and 14 show you have strong spending characteristics. In which area did you have the most yes answers?

| Saver | Spender |
|---|---|
| 1. ____ | 4. ____ |
| 2. ____ | 5. ____ |
| 3. ____ | 6. ____ |
| 8. ____ | 7. ____ |
| 9. ____ | 13. ____ |
| 10. ____ | 14. ____ |
| 11. ____ | |
| 12. ____ | |

| Total yes _____ | Total yes _____ |
|---|---|

Now, what does the quiz show? Are you a saver or a spender? I'll bet that you already know which financial personality type your child or children are. Just to make sure, though, take one more short quiz and see:

## THE CHILD'S FINANCIAL PERSONALITY TYPE QUIZ

1. If you give your child money, does he or she save it?
   Yes _____    No _____
2. Does your child lose or misplace money often?
   Yes _____    No _____
3. Do you often hear the words "I want, I want" when you go shopping with your youngster?
   Yes _____    No _____
4. If you ask your young one, "Why do you want this?" does he or she often say, "Because Johnny has one" or "I saw it on TV"?
   Yes _____    No _____
5. Is your child reluctant to spend any of his or her own money?
   Yes _____    No _____
6. Does your child get exceptional pleasure in seeing a bank account grow?
   Yes _____    No _____
7. If your child sees a penny on the ground, will he go out of his way to pick it up?
   Yes _____    No _____
8. Does your child decide to save for a special toy, and then later choose not to buy the toy?
   Yes _____    No _____
9. If you say no to the suggestion of stopping for ice cream or pizza, does your child ask, "Can we if I pay for it?"
   Yes _____    No _____
10. When you travel, does your youngster want to bring presents back to all her friends?
    Yes _____    No _____

How to Score: Yes answers to questions 1, 5, 6, 7, and 8 indicate you have a saver on your hands. A yes answer to questions 2, 3, 4, 9, and 10 show you have a full-fledged spender in the family. Which of the two personality types is your child?

| *Saver* | *Spender* |
|---------|-----------|
| 1. ____ | 2. ____ |
| 5. ____ | 3. ____ |
| 6. ____ | 4. ____ |
| 7. ____ | 9. ____ |
| 8. ____ | 10. ____ |
| Total yes _____ | Total yes _____ |

Okay. Now you know which way your child leans when it comes to money, and what kind of an influence you will be on him. Stay calm. Even if one of you scored very high in one category or the other, indicating either a Silas Marner pinchpenny or a free-for-all spender, there are adjustments that can greatly temper these predispositions toward the extreme.

The ideal financial personality, of course, is right in the middle: a careful spender *and* a disciplined saver. This is what we will be working on in this book.

The way we will do this is not by using whips and chains to change the youngster's behavior (at least not right away). Instead, I will show you how to help your offspring set specific short-range and long-range goals for their money. The excitement of pursuing these goals and then the satisfaction of attaining them will begin to instill in your child the true joy of money.

# 2 How to Teach Your Child the Basics of Money Management

What is the most important concept to teach children about money? Most of us would say "saving money" because it's so hard for many adults to do. Yet that answer is only half right. Teaching children to save money is very important; showing children how to spend money wisely is equally vital.

The average American saves between 4 and 6 percent of his or her annual salary. That leaves, even after taxes, better than 65 percent or more of the salary that must be carefully managed so that all costs of living are covered. One task is no less difficult than the other.

In this book I will focus on how you can teach, inspire, and coax your child into saving money, as well as how to show a young person to examine, evaluate, and choose the ways to spend money intelligently.

> **FACT:** *America has the lowest savings rate of any industrialized nation. It ranks 21 out of 24 in the world. Here is a 1991 study that shows Net Household Savings as a Percentage of Disposable Household Income by country:*
> 1. *Portugal*
> 2. *Greece*
> 3. *Italy*
> 4. *Belgium*
> 5. *Ireland*

Source: O.E.C.D. Economic Outlook 1992, Steve Malin, Federal Reserve Bank of New York.

## *Where to Start*

Saving money is essentially a discipline that youngsters must be taught just like brushing their teeth or doing their homework. Think about this first process. You provide the child with the *tools* needed: a toothbrush and toothpaste; then you provide the *proper environment*, a bathroom with a sink, to practice the discipline; and, finally, you *monitor the activity* and *offer encouragement and praise* for successfully completing the newly learned task.

I will offer here a similar three-step process for teaching children how to save money. Be prepared. Teaching kids how to spend money wisely is much more complicated and will consume a considerable portion of this book. Unless your offspring is a teenager, though, learning how to save money is the place to start.

The very first step is to explain to your child what *money* is. Here is an appropriate definition for a young child:

**MONEY:** *Anything a group of people accept in exchange for goods or services.*

Now, let's explain what *saving* means. Here is a young child's definition:

**SAVING:** *Saving means putting something away in a safe place to be used, if needed, at another time.*

We all save something (besides money) to use at another time. Squirrels save nuts to eat during the winter; mothers save dessert until after dinner; and more and more people are saving empty bottles and aluminum cans for recycling.

---

## THINGS PEOPLE SAVE TO USE LATER

| | | |
|---|---|---|
| Baby clothes | Gift boxes | Safety pins |
| Books | Newspapers | Videotapes |
| Buttons | Pictures | Wedding dresses |

---

## Why Save Money?

We save money for three reasons: first, for protection in case of an emergency; second, for retirement; and third, to buy something we really want. Many people feel that one should save money with the intention of never, ever touching those funds except in the most severe emergency. This is a valid concept, and one that will be addressed later in this book. But first, consider emphasizing the sheer *fun* of saving money to your child. It just might get him or her hooked for life!

For younger children, I suggest that you approach the subject of saving with reason number three—to save for something they really want to buy.

## THINGS ADULTS SAVE MONEY FOR

| | | |
|---|---|---|
| Babies | Education | Jewelry |
| Boats | Furniture | Retirement |
| Cars | House repairs | Stereo |
| Clothes | Houses | Vacations |

As a parent, keep in mind that there are few joys in life more satisfying than earning your own money and then buying something you really want with it. Don't you remember the satisfaction you enjoyed when you bought your first stereo or car or house? Parents can show their children this joy at a very young age, and it will become a gift their kids will benefit from all their lives.

## The Three-Step Approach to Saving Money

No matter how old your child is, if he's still living under your roof, it's not too late for you to begin teaching him how to save money.

I should point out here that my financial developmental scale is a little different from Dr. Spock's. By the time youngsters are in their early teens, they should be earning a significant portion of their own money outside the home (from baby-sitting, cutting lawns, and so forth). In addition, by age fifteen or sixteen, most teenagers are capable of handling *all* their financial affairs (with your supervision) and should be earning most or all of their own "income."

However, just as I wouldn't suggest putting a sixteen-year-old who has never ridden a horse on Secretariat, I am not recommending that you hand over checkbooks and credit cards to your financially naive teenager. Whatever age your child is, start with the basics, the first of which is saving money.

The principles of inspiring anyone (including adults) on how to save money are the same for a youngster age six or sixteen. The general approach to teaching the discipline of saving money is to (1) set a financial goal with your youngster; (2) help him or her earn the money necessary over a period of time to attain that goal; and then (3) enjoy the reward of attaining the goal together. Here are the three specific steps to start a successful savings program:

## HOW TO SET UP A SAVINGS PROGRAM

1. *Provide your child with the tools to save.* They must have a source of money, preferably earned, that enables them to have money of their own to save (details on how and when to start an allowance are in Chapter 3).
2. *Provide the proper environment where the child can safely keep the money saved.* This can be a piggy bank or toy safe.
3. *Monitor the activity and provide encouragement.* Set attainable goals and then reward your child with praise for successfully saving the money.

Remember that saving money regularly is a habit that requires some measure of self-discipline—but who do you know who has an unending supply of that? Don't set up a system that relies too heavily on your child's ability to discipline himself. It can only fail in the long run.

Instead, provide your offspring with a simple, easy-to-use system to save money so that it becomes a weekly habit. Pay the allowance in exact change and at the same time each week. Make sure the youngster has a special, safe place to keep the money. If the child is saving up for something, tape a picture of the item on the piggy bank as a reminder.

The easier it is for the youngster to get into the habit of

saving money, the less pressure there will be on her self-discipline—and that will be a relief to you both!

Since my principal mandate is to make learning fun, I will be suggesting games and exercises for you to do with your youngster. Remember that these activities are only designed to prime the pump and generate interest. With or without weekly games and incentives, your child still needs a basic ongoing savings plan—until he has the first trillion dollars safely locked up!

Here are specific suggestions on working with your child at her age level. Before you skip to your youngster's age, make sure he or she understands the basics discussed at younger levels. You may also want to do a quick review of these before starting.

### AGES 2 TO 4.

For very young children, you first may need to explain what money is before you talk about saving it (see a young child's definition of money earlier in this chapter, page 23).

Here are three What Is Money? games to further familiarize your offspring with coins. Each exercise is designed to help young ones learn to recognize coins and to develop simple reading, memory, and reasoning skills as well. The games can be played at the kitchen table while you prepare dinner, or in a doctor's waiting room, or even in the car on a long trip.

This first game, the Coin Identification Game, is designed to teach young ones how to recognize coins and their value.

## THE COIN IDENTIFICATION GAME

**GOAL:**
To teach the youngster how to identify a coin three ways: by its size, its name, and its number or value.

**TOOLS:**

Paper, pencil, and several coins, including at least one penny, nickel, dime, quarter, half-dollar, and one-dollar coin (if you can find one). Trace each coin on the paper and, under the circle, write out the name of the coin and its denomination (for example, "Quarter = 25 cents").

**RULES:**

Call out the name of a coin (penny, dime, etc.) and see if your child can select the correct coin from the pile of coins and put it on the right circle.

Note that some coins have more than one name. On the coins themselves, a penny is called "one cent," a nickel is called "five cents," and a fifty-cent piece is called a "half-dollar," so use those descriptions in addition to the common names when you write them down.

**HOW TO WIN:**

The child wins if he can place the entire pile of coins on their correct circles.

---

The next exercise will introduce your young one to the relationship of coins to one another. For instance, five nickels also equals one quarter.

---

## THE SMALL-CHANGE GAME

**GOAL:**

To show a child how to count money and understand its value.

**TOOLS:**

First, conduct a treasure hunt with your child to gather up all the loose change in the house. Don't forget the pockets of coats and jackets, drawers, old purses, and under sofa cushions!

**RULES:**

At the kitchen table, help your little one divide the "treasure" into piles of pennies, nickels, dimes, and so forth.

### HOW TO WIN:

See how many different combinations of coins your child can create that add up to $1. Are there twenty nickels? Or are there ten nickels and two quarters? If the child comes up with three or more different combinations, she wins!

Your youngster is bound to be impressed with what one hundred pennies piled in front of him looks like. This is a good moment to emphasize the value of a dollar and perhaps how hard someone, like a parent, works to earn it.

After you've finished the game, show your child how to "roll" the coins into the paper tubes that banks use (most banks will give you these free). After each group of coins is counted, help the child add up the total. Is there enough "treasure" to send out for a pizza?

### AGES 5 TO 8.

Get a piggy bank that is just for savings; spending money should go somewhere else, like a coin purse or wallet. Each week when you pay out the allowance, go with your child and together "deposit" money into the piggy bank.

> **TIP TO PARENTS:** *Make sure the piggy bank (or jar) is clear so the child can see how the money accumulates each week. Have fun with your child watching it "grow"!*

Many youngsters in this age range can handle the next game, the Quick-Change Game. Making change, or checking to see that you received the correct change back after a purchase, is a difficult task for a youngster (and some adults!) because it requires the customer to do some quick, on-the-spot arithmetic, and usually while under considerable pressure from those around him.

This kitchen table game is designed to gently introduce your child to the concept of making change in a pressure-free environment.

The quick-change exercise is valuable in another way. You will notice that counting money is very different from counting numbers. A young child may have the ability to count up to one hundred, but have trouble counting out the change from a purchase made with a $20 bill.

Why? Because giving change is done very differently. Sometimes the change giver starts in the middle of the equation ("Your total is $3.80, so here's twenty cents and one dollar makes five") or at the end and works backward ("You gave me five dollars, so your change is $1.20 for a $3.80 purchase").

## THE QUICK-CHANGE GAME

**GOAL:**

To show the youngster how to give and receive correct change.

**TOOLS:**

First, take five dollars' worth of change and divide it into four small, shallow boxes, one each for pennies, nickels, dimes, and quarters. This will be your imaginary cash register.

Then, put together a bag of grocery items. Make sure that each item has a price tag on it, or mark it with a price if it needs one.

**RULES:**

To start the game, you will be the customer and your child will be the cashier. With a $5 bill, choose one item that you will pretend to buy from your cashier-child.

Give your child the single item and the $5 bill, and help her give you back the correct change. Take turns being cashier and customer.

Then gradually expand the number of purchases from one item to several. Include a product that is priced at "3 for $1" and explain to the youngster why a store will round off the price to 34 cents when purchased singly.

Be inventive and use different situations with your child. For instance, when you are the customer, you might try intentionally purchasing more than your $5 allotment, and then figure out with the cashier-child what you must put back to stay under the $5. (Generally, this is considered a fairly humiliating experience when it happens in real life, but it is good mathematical practice for your youngster.)

**HOW TO WIN:**
See who can pick out the most groceries without going over the $5.

## Teaching Personal Values through Money

What do you do in real life if a cashier gives you back too much money? Do you return it or keep it? What would you want your child to do?

The Quick-Change Game can be an opportunity to discuss this issue of honesty with your child and review your personal values with your youngster. Be sure to include what the consequences might be to the busy cashier who makes an honest mistake. Could the mistake cost him his job? Or maybe the cashier must make up the deficit out of his own pocket?

Also, talk with your child about how to handle a situation where the cashier does not give you back enough change. As a former bank president, I can tell you that most professional money handlers are trained to verbally *and* physically count out the change they are putting in your hand. In real life, especially outside a bank, this isn't the way it always happens.

If a cashier or clerk simply puts bills and coins in your hand without counting them out, I suggest that all consumers, adult or child, make a habit of the following:

## HOW TO RECEIVE CHANGE FROM A CLERK OR CASHIER

1. Don't leave the immediate area until you've counted the change yourself *in sight* of the cashier. If there is a mistake, it's almost impossible to rectify the situation once you've moved away.
2. If there is a mistake and you've been short-changed, stay at the cashier area and bring the discrepancy to the attention of the cashier immediately.
3. Be polite. Don't automatically assume this person is attempting to steal from you. Most often, it is an honest mistake. And don't forget that it could be *your* mistake or something else entirely. Perhaps the item's price is incorrectly marked.
4. If the problem is not rectified, ask the cashier to call for a manager or supervisor. This brings in a (theoretically) objective third party to mediate. Politely and unemotionally explain the situation and ask for the manager's intervention. In some retail facilities, there is the option of "ringing out the register" to match the total sales for the day with the cash in the drawer. This can verify if there is too much money in the drawer for the total sales, thus justifying your claim of too little change. Obviously, this is a disruptive and time-consuming process, but if your $50 bill was mistaken for a $20 bill, it is worth it.
5. If this fails, your only recourse may be to write a letter to the head of the company. Be sure to include the exact date, time, and names of the people involved, plus a Xerox of your register receipt, in your correspondence.

**CONSUMER TIPS:** *Two tips to help safeguard yourself from mistakes: First, if you are handing a cashier a large bill, like a $20 bill or a $50 bill, say out loud,*

*"Here is a $50 bill."* It helps to call attention to the denomination.

*Second, keep an eye on the monitor as the cashier runs your purchases over the electronic eye that reads prices. Sometimes the true prices of items on sale are not properly recorded in the computer register. You may not remember every price, but you should catch any major irregularities, like "3.00" instead of ".30" for limes.*

## AGES 9 TO 12.

Many parents open savings accounts for their children when they are born. Such accounts, known as custody accounts, are held jointly in the name of the parent and the child. If you did not open such an account in a bank when your child was born, now is the time.

Check with your bank—most banks encourage "total relationship banking," which means that all of a family's balances added together count toward meeting the bank's minimum balance requirements. Your child's account, no matter how small, would be part of this "total relationship."

Nowadays, the most common kind of savings account is statement savings, but many banks still offer passbook accounts. A passbook account is more fun for your child because the passbook is stamped every time there is a deposit. If your bank offers only statement savings accounts, show your child his statement when you receive it.

My children opened accounts at a much younger age, but that was largely due to their following me into work at the bank. For many kids, even age four or five is not too young to understand about savings accounts.

As with younger children, go with an older child each week to deposit his money, confirm his total balance, and share in his excitement at watching the amount grow. (See Chapter 5 for more banking specifics.)

After the initial excitement that comes from opening a first savings account, you may want to devise a follow-up project that solidifies the joy of saving with your child.

Together with your child, select a toy, game, or book that costs no more than two weeks of allowance. (If your youngster is under nine, consider "visiting" the toy after one week to encourage her interest.) Then at the end of the two weeks, make a special trip with her to purchase the item. Be enthusiastic and express your pleasure at her ability to save money.

Build on that small success. Suggest to your child that she try increasing the saving time to four weeks for a second, more expensive item. Set one-month goals for a while, then gradually move to two months, and so on.

Generally with young ones, say three to seven years old, their tastes are not yet as expensive as those of kids a bit older. If you get to the one-month sum, and that amount covers the cost of most toys, keep this time frame for a while to solidify the habit of saving and reward.

As you set longer-term saving goals for your child, what may happen is the youngster no longer wants the item for which he has been saving for over two months. That's okay! And it's an important lesson in consumerism: time can determine how much you really want something.

### AGES TWELVE AND UP.

Consider turning over to your teenager complete management of her clothing allowance, or the total amount of money you spend annually on him. (See Chapter 8 for more details.)

## What to Do with Reluctant Savers

Let's say you've established a weekly allowance (aka salary) for your youngster with assigned chores, and you've provided the child with a place to put his earnings, but putting money in savings, or keeping it there, is not working. What can you do?

Clearly, you've got a spender on your hands. Don't panic yet; there are many adjustments and incentives a parent can try to modify this behavior. It may not be easy, but a spender can be taught to save money.

First, find out why the youngster continues to dip into his savings. Perhaps there has been a series of family birthdays or holidays, such as Mother's Day and Father's Day, that have depleted the child's savings, and it's therefore a temporary situation. Or maybe there are additional expenses—more notebook paper, more food for lunch—that are not covered in the budget.

If the kid is dipping into savings to cover unanticipated expenses, then there needs to be an adjustment in the budget. You need to work with your child to figure out how these unexpected expenses can be covered. However, if the youngster is intoxicated with her newfound spending capabilities, then you, the parent, must take action quickly.

Think about what adults do to inspire or discipline themselves to save money. For many people, "out of sight is out of mind." Perhaps the clear money jar that the younger child is using needs to be moved into a drawer or closet out of temptation. Or maybe it needs to be moved to your closet or drawer for safekeeping.

For an older child, you be the banker for the savings. Use a little notebook to keep a running balance written down for the child. Then, when your offspring wants to take money out of savings for something, he must come to you and discuss it before he can get the cash.

If, after the two of you have discussed a possible purchase, you feel the child should not spend this money, put a week's moratorium on the account. Since most spenders get into trouble with impulse buying, the chances are great that the youngster will forget about the purchase after a week's time. However, if he doesn't and still wants the money, and you still feel it is an inappropriate expenditure, guess who wins? You, the parent, get the final say. (Hey, who said life is fair?)

Those are easy adjustments. Here are two more solutions that are a bit more drastic:

## THE PAYROLL DEDUCTION PLAN.

For third-degree spenders, a parent might consider setting up a "payroll deduction plan" where you, the parent and "employer," withhold the designated savings sum each week out of the kid's allowance. After one month, show the youngster how much he or she has accumulated and emphasize that in another month the amount will be twice as much. Usually, the sight of such a nice, fat nest egg converts the youngster into an enthusiastic saver.

For older kids and teenagers, consider this savings incentive:

## THE 401(k) SAVINGS PLAN.

This works the same way for youngsters as adults. Explain to your child that for every dollar (or whatever amount you determine) he saves, you will match it with a dollar for whatever period of time you decide.

This can be an ongoing incentive, or done on a project-by-project basis, such as when helping your teenager buy his first bicycle or car.

It is valuable to emphasize to the youngster that a 401(k) plan is viewed by most employers as a benefit, or something that is given as reward for good work.

## What to Do with Relentless Savers

As hard as it is to believe, relentless saving can be as inappropriate as uncontrollable spending. However, since it creates less immediate and obvious damage, a parent may be less concerned with reforming the compulsive saver.

Long-term compulsive savers will get themselves into trouble just as free-for-all spenders will. A compulsive saver can become a master at either avoiding payment or manipulating others to give him money. Compulsive savers make difficult partners (business or matrimonial) as adults.

People who hoard money are rare, but not unheard of. I've known a few in my time and some were young children. I remember a favorite cousin who lived near us and whom we enjoyed playing with as youngsters. Doug was always saving his money for something special, which was admirable, except that every time we wanted to go to the movies or for ice cream, Doug would refuse because he didn't want to spend his allowance. He was quite stalwart under enormous peer pressure from my sisters and me. In the end, we almost always ended up paying for him just because we liked his company, but his behavior was manipulative.

For some extreme savers, hoarding is not a love of saving but rather a fear of spending. They may believe (erroneously) that people who spend money are bad and those who save good. Keep an eye out for unusual behavior, and talk to your child about his feelings if you think his is excessive. Explain that the key to managing money successfully is finding a proper balance between spending and saving.

My philosophy is this: *Money should be fun!* You don't play with an entire paycheck, but even when I've been on the tightest of budgets, I've tried to set aside just a few dollars that I could spend on the most whimsical of things, whether it's popcorn for the pigeons in the park or my favorite bubble bath.

Keep an eye out for the signs of a compulsive saver. The phrase "save for a rainy day" will not be an old cliché to your saver if on a rainy Saturday afternoon when everyone is stuck indoors the family decides to combine their resources to pay for a trip to the movie theater or video rental store.

The reality is that all of us, children and adults, may have *moments* of uncontrollable spending and compulsive saving. It's much like falling off your diet: you hope you don't do too much damage, and the next day you try to go back on the diet. Balance, then, is the operative word here for parents.

# 3 *When to Start Your Child on an Allowance*

*C*hild development experts have debated for generations over the value or harm of giving young children a weekly allowance and, if given, at what age. My response to this burning issue? "Yes," and "Beginning at age three."

When children understand that Mommy and Daddy go to the store and buy things with money, then they are ready to start to learn more about money. Usually children pick up on this relationship between money and buying things at a young age. To check, ask your child: "What do Mommy or Daddy do with money in a store?" If they understand that it takes money to be able to leave the store with merchandise, then they are ready to begin with the following money management techniques.

The goal of this book is to help you teach your

children about money management. To do that, youngsters must have real money of their own to manage. Rather than handing a youngster a sizable sum of money, or doling it out a dollar at a time, a weekly allowance gives the child a source of income that he or she can learn to make decisions about.

I will focus more specifically on the size of the allowance later in this chapter, but in general, the sum needs to be large enough so the kid can do all the money management exercises that will prepare her for the future. (Be prepared: the fifty cents a week that you got as a child won't enable your offspring to learn much about finance today!)

The second heated debate concerning allowances is about whether this weekly money should be tied to chores. Yes, yes, yes! In addition to using an allowance to teach money management, this weekly sum will also show your child the relationship between work (chores) and money (allowance), clearly an important concept. Not only will the child someday work for money, but earning an allowance will underscore the fact that you, the parent, work hard for your money, too.

Before getting into how much allowance to give, and when and where to give it, let's go over the decisions you have to make as a parent before you start an allowance, or, if you are already giving your child an allowance, how you can restructure it to enable her to manage different aspects of finance.

## *What Decisions a Parent Must Make Before Starting an Allowance*

Certainly there are ways of teaching money management other than the allowance "earn-and-learn" structure. They will be covered as we go along. None, I believe, is as meaningful to the child as the hands-on system of managing an allowance.

Before we start, here are the questions you need to ask yourself:

1. Can I afford to pay my child a weekly allowance?
2. Is my child old enough to begin learning about money and responsibility?
3. What household chores do I want to tie to the payment of an allowance?

## How to Determine the Amount of the Allowance

Once you've decided that an allowance is a useful teaching tool and that your child—even one as young as three—is ready to begin "earning and learning," then you need to formulate a starting "salary."

For my own two children, I started them on an allowance when they were three and six years old. I used an easy rule of thumb: their allowance was the same number of dollars as their age. I've continued to use this rule as they've grown.

Many people's first reaction is that three dollars is a lot of money for a three-year-old. Let me explain what you and your youngster will be doing with this money.

There are three basic areas of money management we will be working on in this book. I call it my S.O.S. system. Briefly, they are:

1. *Savings.* Some portion of the allowance needs to be allotted for both short-term savings, like for a special toy or outing, and long-term savings, such as for a bicycle or college fund.
2. *Offerings.* This is a small amount of money set aside for donations to charity or to the less fortunate. However small the sum, it is a valuable way for a parent to teach personal values through money by showing the child how to share her good fortune.
3. *Spending.* Depending on the budget you develop with your child, part of her spending money may go to cover specific expenses. It can range from lunch money or bus fare for young ones, to total management of a year's clothing budget for more sophisticated teenagers. At any age, how-

ever, there needs to be some money that is the child's discretionary fund to spend as he wishes (with whatever limitations you set, for example, no drugs, no candy, no automatic assault weapons).

Think about your own financial priorities. What percentage of your budget goes to saving, to charity, and to spending? Would you want your child's priorities to be similar to or different from yours? For example, would you like to see your offspring save more (percentagewise) than you are able to? If areas such as saving and charitable giving are important to you, then you may need to increase the amount of the allowance for the youngster to accomplish this.

## Giving to Charity

Charitable giving is a subject close to my heart and something that I have emphasized to my children since they were young. It is a lesson with great impact to a child or young adult and, again, is an opportunity for you to impart your personal values to your youngster.

Charitable donations can be made in many ways, from giving change to a homeless person on the street (a powerful visual lesson to a child, seeing that there are those obviously less fortunate), to giving to a specific charity that you and the child pick out together. There are many wonderful child-oriented not-for-profit programs, like Ronald McDonald House or—one of my favorites—UNICEF. These and many other organizations welcome kids giving to kids.

This "offering" fund does not have to be limited to traditionally defined charitable organizations or needy individuals. Perhaps you and your child prefer supporting other causes, such as protecting the environment or an endangered species like the whales.

Another alternative is to donate money to general-giving organizations that distribute the funds where they are most needed; such organizations include the Salvation Army, the Red Cross, and the United Way. Also, many churches and synagogues have programs for assisting the needy.

Remember that charity can also mean giving of yourself and your time as well as money. For instance, some people volunteer their time to work in a soup kitchen or read to the blind. Your youngster might want to consider recycling some of his or her clothes or toys that are in good condition to the Salvation Army or a local children's hospital.

This is a good dinner table discussion to have with your child or children. Find out where their interests are. You might be surprised at what you find out!

Share with your children all ways money can work positively: it works to cover immediate expenses, like lunch money; it works to build for the future, like saving for college; and it can be shared with others to help those truly in need.

## The S.O.S. Allowance Equation

Back to formulating how much you, the "employer," pay your "employee(s)."

In addition to the allowance-equals-age formula I suggested earlier, there is another way to come up with a figure for the allowance. First, start with spending. Chances are you're already doling out money to your youngster each week for something. Is it milk money or bus fare? Do you regularly allow your young one to pick one special item for himself at the grocery store? Do you give your kid money to go to the movies each week? Do you give him money for Sunday school? Figure out what living expenses you are currently paying for on a regular basis and consider turning over those responsibilities to your child.

Now you have added up a weekly spending figure. Next, how much money would you like to see the child put in savings each week? Add that to the spending figure. Finally, add 10 to 15 percent of this sum for charitable offerings, and you should have a total allowance that is workable.

---

### THE S.O.S. ALLOWANCE EQUATION

---

Savings + Spending = X
10 to 15% of X = Y
(multiply X times .10 to .15 for percentage)
X + Y (charitable offerings) = Total Allowance

---

I lay out examples of this equation with specific numbers in the next chapter.

## Chores and Allowance

The last question that you will need to answer before you introduce your child to an allowance (or adjust the allowance you are already paying out) concerns the subject of chores. What job or jobs must the youngster perform in order to earn the allowance? And, separately, what duties are part of the child's role as a member of the family, or, as I like to call it, a citizen of the household?

I believe in assigning specific chores that the child does weekly to earn the allowance. This does not include such things as helping me bring in the bags of groceries from the car or listening for the telephone while I take a bath. I like to differentiate additional responsibilities from routine courtesies.

In my household, we have two kinds of chores: personal maintenance (like keeping one's bedroom free from diseases and fire hazards) and general household chores (such as setting the table or dusting the living room furniture). Payment of the allowance is based on the latter. Each child has specific chores that must be completed each week before the allowance is paid.

The first point to make to a young child when you are just starting an allowance is that this weekly sum of money is not an "entitlement program"—parents do not owe their children spending money. Instead, an allowance is money given to the child as payment for being a working, contributing member of the family.

Also, it should be reassuring to you to keep in mind that you will not have to pay out an allowance for the rest of the child's life. (After all, $43 a week is a big chunk of change for someone on a fixed income!) Actually, the weekly allowance should start adjusting downward as your youngster heads into his teens and begins to earn his own money.

### How to Choose and Implement Chores

Again, as you did with the youngster's expenses, jot down what chores your child is currently doing. Then, think about what extra duties you feel she could handle now that she is "employed."

My experience has been that it is more effective in the long run if you allow the child to choose some of the assigned duties. For my kids, I had two or three mandatory chores (clean the bedroom, take dirty clothes to the laundry) and then they could select a household job from a list that I had made up. (The list included things like dusting the living room, tying up old newspapers into a neat bundle, emptying all the wastepaper baskets.) Allowing the child some input into the decision-making process here makes him an active participant and a more enthusiastic one.

If there is more than one child in the house, and they

are close in age and ability, you might try rotating jobs occasionally. This job rotation technique goes a long way in avoiding gender casting of jobs. After all, girls do need to know how to take out the garbage and boys are perfectly capable of whipping up a salad for dinner!

There needs to be flexibility on both sides. For instance, maybe the child's assignment is to dust the living room furniture by noon on Saturdays before the allowance is paid. However, let's say that this week you're hosting a dinner party on Friday night and could use a dust-free environment. What can you do? Let's hope you have a cooperative "employee" who will accommodate your deadline.

On the other hand, perhaps your daughter, who routinely does her dusting on Saturday mornings, gets a last-minute invitation to a slumber party and probably won't get home until later on Saturday afternoon. Now it is the parent's turn to be understanding.

It is, however, the child's responsibility to inform you when he sees that he can't meet his deadline. If, for any reason short of sudden illness or hospitalization, the youngster cannot complete his chores by the assigned time, then he needs to negotiate a new deadline with you.

When a parent should not be flexible is in the payment of the allowance. *The chores must be completed before any money is paid.* Your deal with the child is the same as any employer's, "no work, no pay." This means all chores. Just as you would not pay a painter half his fee for a half-painted house, your child does not get 50 percent of his allowance if only half of his chores have been completed. Stand fast on this.

If the problem of missed deadlines for completing chores becomes chronic, then the parent needs to reevaluate the situation. Is the child carrying more responsibility than she can handle? Is she not budgeting her time so these tasks are completed? Work with your youngster to make the necessary adjustments. Perhaps she does less work and gets less allowance. Any punishment, however, should be financial: no work, no pay. This is not a situation in which the child should be sent to her room or denied television privileges.

Discuss with your youngster what happens if the chores are not completed by the prearranged allowance-paying deadline. I approach each new situation by asking myself, "How would an employer handle this in a fair way with an employee?" This helps me determine a solution that I can then scale down to fit my child.

One suggestion is to make a master Chore Check List for the refrigerator door. It might look like this:

---

## CHORE CHECK LIST

|                          |                             |
| ------------------------:| --------------------------- |
| Chores:                  | Dust living room furniture  |
|                          | Change the cat box          |
|                          | Clean the picture window    |
| Job Assigned to:         | Kyle Godfrey-Fraebel        |
| Deadline for Completion: | Saturday at noon            |
| Completed: ____          | Incomplete: ____            |
| Paid:                    | (date)                      |

---

Remember that it is the wise employer who knows when to promote a worker to a more challenging job. A four-year-old might be able to handle simple dusting duties; a nine-year-old may be ready for more creative or complex endeavors like cooking or lawn care.

My kids occasionally switch jobs just for fun, and, on occasion, have teamed up to work together to get the chores done faster. As long as the work is completed, I have no problem with whatever creative negotiations they conduct between themselves.

## How to Structure an Allowance

Try to structure the allowance you give your child the same way an employer sets up payment of salaries. Decide on a day and place where the allowance is paid, and make every effort to maintain this routine.

Also, be sure to provide your young ones a specific place to keep their money, whether it's a jar, shoebox, or piggy bank. Remember that you will need to pay the allowance out in small bills and change so the "payee" can immediately "deposit" some funds into savings and offerings. More about setting these banks up later.

## How to Explain an Allowance to Your Child

Okay, with piggy bank in hand, you now are ready to explain this exciting, very "grown-up" new program to your young one. Start by describing what an allowance is, and why you think the child is ready to enter the exciting world of money.

Let's start with a young child's definition of allowance:

**ALLOWANCE:** *Money the parent gives a child each week as a payment for being a working member of the family.*

You might want to add that even adults sometimes get an allowance. An adult might have a clothes allowance, a grocery allowance, and even a spending allowance.

Remember my S.O.S. plan? Emphasize that this lump sum of money will have specific purposes. Part of the weekly allowance will automatically go directly into the piggy bank to be saved, another part goes to charitable offerings, and the final chunk is for spending.

## Who Now Pays for What?

The question will come up, and more than once, over who pays for the many unexpected expenses that always emerge during the course of real life. Unfortunately, there are no hard and fast rules to go by here. If, for example, my son suddenly needs $11 for a class trip to see the new Monet exhibit, it's hard for me to say no. If his slightly worn, but still usable sneakers are no longer the latest style, I have far less trouble saying no.

Now that your grade-schooler has his own money, there sometimes is a tendency toward possessiveness of this money. A parent doesn't want to discourage any strong urges to save, but remember that the allowance was designed to cover some expenses.

Below is the developmental Source of Income chart, which outlines where children should be in terms of financial independence at different ages:

---

### SOURCE OF INCOME

| | |
|---|---|
| Ages 3–9: | Allowance |
| Ages 10–15: | Allowance supplemented by outside jobs (baby-sitting, yard work, etc.) |
| Ages 16 and up: | The teenager's outside job covers expenses like dating and gas. All basic necessities are funded by parent in an account the teenager controls. |

---

Additionally, a parent should have certain odd jobs available to the youngster who wants to supplement his allowance the same way some employers offer overtime pay. For little ones, the job might be something like tying up old newspapers into piles to be recycled or cleaning the baseboards. An older youngster could help with big seasonal jobs like cleaning out the garage or sweeping up the ashes in the fireplace. Make a list of the nonurgent jobs you need done with the "overtime" fee you would pay, and post it on the refrigerator. Then when your offspring asks you for a second pair of designer sneakers or money to go ice skating with friends, refer to the list.

Many parents find this method of supplementing the child's income beneficial to both sides. My own mother used it quite successfully with her three daughters and even gave us advances on the promise we would do the job on a specific date. You will decide if this works with your youngster or not.

# 4 How to Help Your Child Set Up a (Successful) Budget

*B*udget. This is a word that most adults rank right up there with dental work and cleaning the oven as most unfavorite responsibilities. Like trying to stay on a diet, almost every adult has struggled at one time or another to live within a budget.

A budget does not have to be an instrument of torture. It is simply an organizing tool designed to help one manage money more effectively. I like to think of a budget as a kind of road map, a plan that gets you from here to your financial goal down the road.

When was the last time you and your spouse formulated a family and household budget? Does it still exist? Does it work for your family? As we did with analyzing your financial personality and your child's, it is valuable to sit down and assess your own budget for the family before you begin with your child's.

## Evaluating Your Budgeting Skills

Think about what works for you personally. Do you build in a small reward for yourself for staying on the monthly budget? Does an automatic payroll savings program work best for you? Do you stay away from the mall or department stores until all credit cards are paid off?

Almost everybody has little games that they play to accomplish the positive goal of staying on a budget. I play very similar games with myself to stay on a diet. I simply don't allow myself to walk down the cookie aisle at the grocery and I will drive four blocks out of my way to avoid passing a Sweet Sue's ice cream store, but if I'm good all week I allow a small indiscretion on the weekend. (By the way, I frequently compare budgets with diets. It is a concept I identify with strongly and I would be hard pressed to choose which is harder to stick to!)

Think about what proven budget-adhering techniques have worked for you and consider how you could translate those principles into behaviors that might help your youngster.

According to most financial planners, adult budgets fail for one of the following reasons: (1) Lack of commitment (aka self-discipline), (2) unrealistic goals, or (3) a serious emergency, such as sudden unemployment, divorce, or illness, that disables the budget.

Reasons number one and two can be fixed. And while you can't anticipate what emergencies might come up, there is a great deal you can do to protect your budget (by saving money) and thus minimize the financial damage if the unforeseen does happen.

Your child, on the other hand, is probably a newcomer to the world of budgets and there is much you can do to safeguard your offspring's budget from the usual adult pitfalls. I will explain these in more detail as we go along.

## Why Is a Budget Important?

"Why?" is a popular, frequently asked question in my household full of young ones, and one I'm sure pops up in your family as well. Before I get into what a budget is and how to set one up for your child, let's discuss why a budget is important.

I tell my children that "a good budget enables you to pay for what you need and save up for what you want." There will be three or four other significant purposes for a budget that I will get into, but covering one's expenses and maybe saving for a special something are the two most appealing to a child.

As a parent, I feel that budgeting strongly encourages a youngster of any age to face the consequences of spending money, and to discipline the urge we all have for instant gratification.

## The Importance of Setting Financial Goals

Before you sit down with your youngster, ask yourself this question: "What financial goals do I want to encourage my child to set at his age?" Would you like your enterprising ten-year-old to start saving for a car? Should your fourteen-year-old daughter contribute to the cost of that expensive summer camp she wants to attend? Do the twins want to visit Grandma in Florida over the spring break?

If there is a big-ticket item that you feel the youngster would appreciate more if they contributed to it, then look at their "long-term spending" column. You will need to decide if you want to increase the child's income/allowance in this area (and add to the list of chores as well).

The same is true with "spending," particularly in living expenses. Think about the money that you regularly shell out to the child for basic expenses like clothes, food, lunch money, school supplies, movies. Is there a regular expense, such as lunch money, that you routinely pay for that you could turn over to your grade-schooler?

Here are some possibilities:

## WEEKLY EXPENSES THAT A CHILD COULD ABSORB

Lunch money

Bus fare

Sunday School donation

Boy Scout/Girl Scout fees

School supplies

School field trips

Finally, sit down and discuss with your offspring what his or her long-range financial goals are. Be prepared. Your young one may surprise you. You may find out for the first time that Johnny or Jane has a secret desire to become an accomplished photographer (an expensive hobby). Or that they want to have their own pool-cleaning service by next summer.

The goals may change from one month to the next and that's fine. If you allow the youngster to dream, then he is bound to be more enthusiastic over the financial plan that will make the dream come true.

## How to Explain and Set Up a Budget

At this point, you have explained the basics of saving, giving to others, and spending to your child (the S.O.S. plan). She has a source of income, or weekly allowance, and now the two of you together will work out a master plan, or a budget, for this money.

Let's start with a simple definition of what a budget is. Here's my definition for a child:

**BUDGET:** *A plan that lays out what you will do with your money.*

You should have your list and your child's list of financial goals. Additionally, the two of you should make a list of all possible ways the youngster spends money. Be sure to include things like gifts, Saturday matinees and popcorn, and gerbil food.

Now, with your lists of goals and expenses, sit down with her and a piece of paper. Divide the paper vertically into three parts. Under the first third, write the word "Savings," then "Offerings" under the next, and "Spending" under the third—"S.O.S."

Now divide the Savings column in half. Mark one part "Short-term Savings" and the second part "Long-term Savings." Long-term savings is money your child puts away and is used only under an extreme emergency or for a specific long-term goal. Perhaps you designate these funds for a high-ticket item like college or a car, or maybe it is true saving that is not intended for use.

Short-term savings are, obviously, for short-term projects. This includes some "disposable income" for your youngster plus whatever obligations you, the parent, laid out when you started the weekly allowance (see Chapter 3).

For instance, who now pays for Mother's Day, Father's Day, birthday, and holiday gifts? If you've built this into the child's allowance so that he or she covers these things, then the funds are held in short-term savings.

Offerings, or charitable giving, is fairly straightforward. This is a specific sum that you and your youngster have allocated for this purpose. There are a couple of ways you might distribute this money, either weekly or in one lump sum a month to the charity.

Start by deciding with the child which charity should receive the monies. Here are some possibilities:

---

## CHILD-ORIENTED CHARITIES

---

Ronald McDonald House    March of Dimes    Save the Children
UNICEF                         Phoenix House     One to One

---

There may be appropriate outlets through school, church, or synagogue that are meaningful to the youngster. Or maybe there is a charity that relates to the youngster or someone the child knows, such as multiple sclerosis or juvenile diabetes.

Charitable giving or sharing can include cause-related organizations geared toward the homeless, the environment, or education.

Talk about giving to charity with your child. Again, this is where your personal values are reflected, and where you want to direct your youngster's values.

Some children have very strong feelings about who they would like to help with a financial contribution. The more involved your youngster is in the selection of the charitable giving outlet, the more committed she will be to contributing part of the allowance each week.

Now, spending. Again divide this category into two parts. The first will be expenses the youngster must cover—lunch money, bus fare, school supplies, church collection, whatever living expenses you are turning over to the child. The second part will be discretionary money that is used by the child as he wishes.

Your divided piece of paper should look something like this:

## SAMPLE NUMBER 1:
## BREAKDOWN OF A CHILD'S BUDGET

| 1. Savings | 2. Offerings | 3. Spending |
|---|---|---|
| Long-term Savings<br>20% | 10–15% | Living Expenses<br>40% |
| Short-term Savings<br>10–15% | | "Free" Money<br>20% |

Now you and your offspring are ready to divide up the weekly allowance like a pie.

Let's say your child is seven years old and has a weekly allowance of $7. This is how the budget would break down:

## SAMPLE NUMBER 2:
## BREAKDOWN OF A CHILD'S BUDGET

| | 1. Savings | 2. Offerings | 3. Spending |
|---|---|---|---|
| | Long-term Savings<br>$1.40 | .70 | Living Expenses<br>$ 2.80 |
| | Short-term Savings<br>.70 | | "Free" Money<br>$ 1.40 |
| Weekly<br>Totals | $2.10 | .70 | $ 4.20 |
| Monthly<br>Totals | $8.40 | $2.80 | $16.80 |

This is what the budget might look like for an eleven-year-old earning an $11-per-week allowance:

## SAMPLE NUMBER 3:
## BREAKDOWN OF A CHILD'S BUDGET

|  | 1. Savings | 2. Offerings | 3. Spending |
|---|---|---|---|
|  | Long-term Savings | | Living Expenses |
|  | $ 2.20 | 1.10 | $ 4.40 |
|  | Short-term Savings | | "Free" Money |
|  | $ 1.10 | | $ 2.20 |
| Weekly Totals | $ 3.30 | $1.10 | $ 6.60 |
| Monthly Totals | $13.20 | $4.40 | $26.40 |

Now you have the skeleton of a budget. The next step is for you and your child to make whatever adjustments you feel are important.

For instance, the 70 cents a week set aside by the seven-year-old for charitable offerings may not seem like a lot, but it adds up to $36.40 over a year's time. Keep in mind that the point of the offering is to start your child on a *lifelong habit* of giving to charity. (She does not have to endow an entire wing of the children's hospital this year!)

Take a look at savings and spending. These are the harder areas. Is your youngster putting away what he needs to be saving? Is the child getting enough spending money to cover the living expenses he has been assigned?

Start with savings and work down from there. Remember that the purpose of the budget is to *plan for the future,* so long-term savings need to be the untouchable, sacred-cow part of the budget.

The next important area is living expenses. This is a specific amount of money that comes in each week via the allowance, and leaves before the next week's allowance. (I'll address what to do with leftover expenses shortly.)

Now that you have the basic S.O.S. down, see what the figure is that you have left. This will be what you divide between short-term savings and free money, which is the youngster's discretionary fund to use as she wishes. How the division is made will depend on what demands on the money you and the child have laid out.

For instance, something like the Saturday-matinee-and-popcorn expense could conceivably go under either the free money section of the budget or short-term savings. My feeling is that it should go under free money because you don't want the child dipping into savings, even short-term savings, on a regular basis. Short-term savings is designed for just that—saving.

One more important word about the free, discretionary fund. It may be very difficult for you, the parent, to allow the child to make her own decisions on how to use this money, particularly if you feel she's being wasteful. However, try to stay calm. Keep in mind that when children blow their hard-earned money on candy that is quickly gone or a toy that breaks as soon as they get home, they learn a valuable lesson in consumerism.

## Handling Unusual Budgetary Circumstances

As an adult, you know very well what happens with "the best laid plans of mice and men . . ." Unusual circumstances that are unforeseeable are always going to appear when you least expect them. The child's teacher suddenly announces she is leaving to get married and the students want to buy a going-away present, or perhaps your daughter wants a special dress for a party.

You will have to work with your youngster on this kind of surprise expense. The system that I use is a permanent list of odd jobs where the child can earn the money for unexpected expenses.

The point of teaching a child about money and its management is to develop and inspire responsibility in the youngster. Generally, if I feel my children have saved and spent their allowance prudently, I am more prone to help them with the unexpected expenses that come up. Sometimes, for instance, I suggest to my son that we split the $11 class trip fee. This enables him to contribute his resources without depleting them, and it makes me feel that I am helping him do something he really wants to do rather than just doling out another freebie.

For both children and adults, there are always many demands for our money. Choosing when and what we spend our money on is a lifelong challenge. If your child is old enough to earn money, then he or she is old enough to begin the decision-making process on how to spend it. You and the child will work this out together on a case-by-case basis.

Sometimes, however, there are unexpected things that happen that we must pay for. If the headlight on the car is smashed, the adult driver must pay for its replacement whether he broke it or not. Similar issues may come up with your youngster. If your son accidentally hits a baseball through a neighbor's window, who pays for it? You or the child?

The best way to defuse a lot of the emotion of these situations is to discuss the concept of "natural consequences" with your child *before* a calamity happens. Talk with the youngster about what she believes is fair, and what her responsibility in the matter should be.

Here is a list of what-ifs that you and your youngster might talk about:

## IF THIS HAPPENED, WHAT WOULD YOU AND YOUR CHILD DO?

Who pays for accidents like breaking a vase, or a neighbor's window?

What happens when a child loses money?
Should your child loan money to others? Borrow money?
What happens if the child does not complete his or her assigned
   household chores to earn the allowance?

You and your child will probably come to the conclusion
that there are some accidents the youngster will have to pay
part of himself. Consider allowing your offspring to work off
a major mishap by performing additional duties, such as cleaning out the basement or garage. The penalty will make just
as strong an impression on him, but be resolved in a shorter
amount of time.

## ODD JOBS CHILDREN CAN DO FOR EXTRA MONEY

Clean out garage or basement
Rake and bag leaves
Scrub grime from bathtub tiles
Reorganize linen closet
Clean outside windows
Paint fences

Clean lawn furniture
Wash car
Baby-sit
Water plants
Answer phone and take messages
Fold laundry

**GIFTS OF MONEY.**

Often grandparents, aunts and uncles, or adult friends send
children money for birthdays, Christmas, Hanukkah, and so
forth. Sometimes the giver has a specific purpose in mind and
will say so. Usually, though, there are no stipulations on the
money.

Here is the general rule I use with my kids: Gifts of money

under $20 go into their free money budget; between $21 and $50, half goes into savings and the other half into spending. Anything over $50 (which is rare), we work out a percentage where the bulk goes into savings, and some is available to the child.

## INHERITANCE.

I use the same rules here as for gifts.

## LEFTOVER LIVING EXPENSES.

Discuss with your youngster what happens to leftover living expenses. If the child is home sick from school one day, does he get to keep the unused lunch money, or does it carry over to the next week? Or if he chooses not to eat lunch, does he get to keep the money?

Generally, if money is leftover from any section, it should be returned to savings. On something like lunch money where the child was out sick or wanted to cram for an upcoming quiz, that specific expense should be subtracted from the next week's allowance.

However, if the youngster is not eating lunch so she can save the money instead, this could be either a budgetary problem or a behavior problem. If she's not eating lunch because she needs the money for other things, you may want to take another look at the budget. Is she not eating lunch in order to meet her other expenses? Or perhaps she's not eating lunch so she can buy more clothes.

Perhaps the child is a compulsive saver or spender. If so, see the section in Chapter 2 for ways to resolve these types of problems. (Don't forget that the kid also has the option of doing odd jobs, which is a better way of earning extra money than starving!)

Most parents would not like the thought of their offspring going hungry at lunch and spending the money on something else. If the youngster was, on the other hand, walking home from school so that he could save the bus fare, would you object to him earning the bus fare?

These are issues you will have to discuss and work out with your youngster.

**LOST MONEY.**

This falls under the same category as accidents. Again, you may wish to advance the youngster the lost money, and have the child repay it to you over a comfortable period of time.

## What to Do if the Budget Is Not Working

You will need to monitor how your youngster is progressing with her budget. You should watch the situation closely the first few weeks, and then check your child's progress every month or so.

The most common problem is when the youngster "borrows" from one fund to support another—sort of the same thing we adults do and call "creative financing." I would allow this on an occasional basis, particularly if he immediately replaces the funds at his next opportunity. What I would strongly discourage is allowing the borrow-from-Peter-to-pay-Paul situation on a regular basis week after week.

If the savings accounts are being tapped too often, one suggestion is to remove the temptation. This is where a savings account in a bank is useful (see Chapter 5). If the bank is not practical, have the child keep savings in a locked strongbox and give you the key, or give the funds to you to hold as the banker.

Removing the temptation may help, or you may have to reevaluate the budget. Is it too complex for the child? You may need to step back and simplify the budget to the bare bones: savings, offerings, and available spending only. Each week when you pay the youngster the allowance, go with him to put away savings and offerings in an untouchable place, and the spending allowance is his to spend. Then slowly rein-state other funds.

Try showing the youngster how to set up a simple, single-entry journal where he can record what money comes in and where it goes out. It helps all of us to see in black-and-white exactly where our money is going.

Another effective—and fun—technique for your budget-breaker is a game. I call it the Bill-Paying Game and I got the idea for this from the wonderful old Irene Dunne movie *I Remember Mama.* Here's how it works:

## THE BILL-PAYING GAME

### GOAL:
To pay all the monthly bills with the allotted money.

### TOOLS:
A dozen envelopes, Monopoly or other kind of play money, the receipts of old bills for utilities, mortgage or rent, telephone bill, insurance, credit cards and department stores, day-care bill, pool-cleaning service, milkman, butcher (any regular monthly household expense).

### RULES:
Count out in the play money what an "average" parent or parents bring home in salary each month. Then mark on the outside of each envelope the total amount due for each bill; for example, telephone, $56, water, $14, MasterCard, $223. Then put money from the salary into each envelope, and see how much is left over.

Point out to the youngster things like "minimum payment due" as opposed to "total balance due," and let the child decide how much to pay on the bill. Also note the "date due" information.

### HOW TO WIN:
Everybody wins if there is money left over after paying all the bills, and everybody loses if there isn't enough money.

If there is money left over, then decide what should be done with the leftover money.

You may feel comfortable enough with your child to play this game for real, using checks to pay your real monthly bills. It is a dramatic way of showing where the family income goes and the difficult decisions you must make.

# 5 How to Introduce Your Child to the World of Banking

As a brilliant, captivating teacher of financial management, you will soon find that your child, being an equally brilliant and cooperative student, has now accumulated a significant amount of money through his or her flawless management of allowances and wages.

Well, even if the youngster hasn't saved a small fortune, it's time to introduce your youngster to the banking system.

Safeguarding this sizable sum by moving it to the bank is only one of many good reasons to begin working with a financial institution. Throughout his or her lifetime, your child will come to utilize many banking services. In addition to the standard savings account, the kid will eventually want a checking account, a credit card, and someday, perhaps a student loan for college, or a car loan, or a mortgage. Six or seven years old is not too young to introduce a child to banking.

A bank is to money management what a grocery store is to cooking or food management. Maybe you prefer to grow all your own fruits and vegetables, but eventually you will want to venture into the supermarket for a little coffee and steak!

## Establishing Your Own Relationship with a Bank

Before I begin talking about your child and banking, let's focus a minute on your own relationship with your bank. Do you have one?

To many parents, the bank may seem like graduate school stuff. Lots of otherwise intelligent and fearless adults are struck by the austerity of a bank. It may seem to some people that bankers speak a foreign language, they keep their personnel behind "cages," there's not much laughter or chitchat, and on top of that, there is a uniformed guard with a sidearm waiting at the door. Outwardly, it is not a friendly environment.

Certainly banks or savings and loans are no place for a party. But in the past few years, banks have recognized their image problem as unapproachable, even intimidating institutions and have made great strides toward becoming more "user friendly." While I was president of The First Women's Bank in New York City, for instance, I softened the colors of the bank lobby and hung original artwork by local artists. Loan officers' desks were easily seen and accessible, not behind partitions or walls. These were small changes, but they reinforced the idea that we were glad the customer was there.

For me, the ideal situation is to have a sort of Marcus Welby, M.D.–type of relationship with your banker that is as active in financial "sickness" as it is in "health." Mr. or Ms. Banker is there to help me through the big situations, like mortgages and loans, and the little ones, like when I forget to write down the amount of a particular check. My Marcus Welby knows me by name and face, and often he can answer a question or take care of a matter for me by telephone.

If you don't have this type of banker, I would encourage you to find one and develop a professional, one-on-one relationship. It takes time and effort, and like a family physician, it needs to be someone you trust and feel comfortable with in discussing the most intimate details of your financial life.

When you have your own Marcus Welby, he becomes a good source to help with your child's banking business. For example, my friend Helen had such a banker, a Mrs. Sears. From the time her daughter was old enough to ride in a stroller, Lizzie accompanied her mother to take care of her banking business. As Lizzie learned to talk, Mrs. Sears would lightly explain to her what she was doing. By the time she was four, Lizzie could fill out a deposit slip with only a little help from Mrs. Sears!

What Mrs. Sears and Helen did very casually as they worked was to explain, in simple terms to Lizzie, what they were doing with money (Helen admits it was more to entertain the youngster than to seriously teach her something). The child, precocious though she was, probably did not understand the activity the first time, but she did eventually, and well enough to do it herself.

The moral of this story is to (again) emphasize the importance of explaining to your youngster what you are doing with money and why. It may seem tedious and even exhausting at times, but the information does seep in, and—if nothing else—it distracts the child from other mischief or boredom.

## How to Explain Banking to Your Child

Hopefully your child already has some idea of what a bank is, even if it has only been in the car with you while you drive through the outdoor teller's window. If not, it's not too soon to introduce her to banks and banking.

First, I will show you how to explain to your youngster what a bank is and how it works. I will go over some basic banking terms and give you simple definitions to help explain these words to your young one. Then I will review what to do on your first official trip to the bank with your child, and finally, I will give suggestions for additional field trips to the bank as your youngster advances.

Let's start with what a bank is, and why we use it.

### Why a Bank Is Better than a Mattress

A hundred years ago, banks were very different from what they are today. First of all, a depositor's money was not insured, so if the bank was robbed or burned down, people lost their deposit and there was little, if anything, they could do about it.

There were also very few banks, particularly west of the Mississippi, so people did what they could to safeguard their cash. Some hid their money in their mattress (a popular place since you knew where it was when you were asleep); others buried it in the backyard. One woman in Colorado by the name of Molly Brown even hid her fortune in her potbellied stove! (The stove idea later proved disastrous when Molly's husband, not knowing the money was there, lit a fire one cold night and burned their entire fortune.)

Fortunately for us, banks are much more plentiful today and far, far safer than stoves or mattresses. In fact, a federally funded government agency known as the Federal Deposit Insurance Corporation (FDIC) insures most banks and their depositors up to $100,000 per person so you can get your money back if it's lost. You can check the door or counter for the FDIC seal to confirm that your bank is insured.

That little bit of information may be comforting to you and your youngster, but the overriding reason for your child to put his money in the bank is for him to take his first step into banking.

A bank is where you care for and maintain your money. Just as you take your car to the gas station to care for and maintain it, and your pets to the vet, the bank is where you take your money to watch over it, cultivate it so it grows, and manage it so it helps you do what you want to do with the money later.

For your children, banking is a real-life activity that they will engage in the rest of their lives. The more they know about a bank and how it works, the better they can utilize banking services and facilities.

Here is a young child's definition of bank:

**BANK:** *A safe place to keep money.*

For kids a bit older (ten and up), you can explain that a bank also is a business, specifically a service (as opposed to a product) business on a scale similar to the post office or a restaurant.

A bank performs a number of services for its customers and, like any for-profit business, it needs to make money. The way most banks make money is to use customers' deposits to lend to other people. When those people pay back the money loaned, they also pay the bank a bit more than they borrowed, and that is called *interest*. The interest the bank earns for itself is profit.

It may be comforting to you and your child to know that there are rules to make sure that the bank doesn't lend out too much money. When a customer wants her money, it is supposed to be there for her.

## RULES FOR BANKS

1. Banks must insure their customers' deposits.
2. Banks must keep a percentage of their deposits in the Federal Reserve Bank.

3. Banks must tell customers the interest on a loan, and how much total interest they will have to pay on a loan.
4. All agreements that bank customers sign must be written in plain English so that the customer understands exactly what it is he or she is signing.
5. Banks may not discriminate against anyone on account of age, sex, religion, race, or ethnic group.
6. Banks should not make loans unless they are sure they will be repaid.

## THE KINDS OF BANKS IN AMERICA

1. *Commercial banks.* This type of bank deals with people and businesses. They offer services like checking and savings accounts and loans. Commercial banks are owned by their stockholders and the profits go to them, if the bank pays dividends.
2. *Thrift banks, savings and loans,* and *credit unions.* All these are very similar. They mostly provide mortgages so people can buy homes. Most savings and loans, credit unions, and thrifts used to be owned by the depositors and the profits were shared among them. But banking is changing, and commercial banks, savings and loans, and thrifts are becoming more alike.
3. *Investment banks.* These are not really banks. They are firms that give investment advice. They also buy and sell stocks and bonds from companies and government agencies and sell smaller quantities of them to investors and individuals at a profit. Investment banks may not accept deposits or make loans.
4. *The central bank of the United States* is called the Federal Reserve System. The Federal Reserve System includes twelve regional Federal Reserve Banks.

## *Beginning Terms for the First-Time Bank Customer*

On your first official trip to a bank with your youngster, you will have two goals: first, to show your child the bank and familiarize him with the surroundings; and second, to open the youngster's first bank account: a savings account.

How do you know when your child is old enough to open a savings account? Well, many parents, or grandparents, open savings accounts in a child's name at birth. They use it to deposit gifts of money to the child, and to build a nest egg for the youngster's future. However, check with your bank on this. Any banking facility will open an account for the child in the parent's name, and some banks will open a savings account for a youngster in his or her own name if the child is old enough to read and write.

> **STATEMENT SAVINGS ACCOUNT:** *A bank account where a bank or savings institution keeps money for you so you can use it at a later date. As long as the money stays in the savings account, the bank pays you interest (but not as much interest as a CD).*

A statement savings account is called that because you get a monthly or quarterly statement in the mail summarizing the activity on your account, as opposed to a passbook savings account where the running balance is tallied in a small book the depositor keeps. The statement savings account is the most common kind of savings account. There are several different kinds of savings accounts, and each pays a different amount of interest.

> **PASSBOOK SAVINGS ACCOUNT.** *Every time you make a deposit or a withdrawal you must present your passbook to the bank for the transaction to be entered. You may also mail your deposit to the bank, and you can*

*send your book along with the deposit so the bank can update the book.*

**CERTIFICATE OF DEPOSIT (CD).** *This is money you deposit for an agreed period of time. Since the bank knows it will have your money for a specific amount of time, it can lend it and not worry about when you will need it. Therefore the bank will pay you a slightly higher rate of interest. If you withdraw your money early, you must pay a penalty.*

**MONEY MARKET ACCOUNT.** *This is similar to a checking account, but it earns interest. Usually you can only write a limited number of checks each month, so the bank pays you a little less interest than a statement savings account.*

**INDIVIDUAL RETIREMENT ACCOUNT (IRA).** *This is a savings account for your retirement. The government allows you to delay paying taxes on the part of your wages that you save in an IRA. If you take the money out early, you pay a penalty and taxes. IRAs can also be other monetary instruments, such as mutual funds.*

**KEOGH ACCOUNT.** *This is like an IRA, but it is for people who are self-employed.*

As far as your child is concerned, we will be focusing on a statement and/or passbook savings account for their first trip to the bank. Take a minute before your field trip to go over the following terms with your youngster. He or she might not understand them completely right away, but start to familiarize your child with them.

**INTEREST:** *Money that is paid to the customer by the bank for keeping the customer's money. Also, interest is* *paid to the bank when the bank lends money to a customer.*

**DEPOSIT:** *The act of putting money into the bank. Also, the sum of money that is put into the bank.*

**WITHDRAWAL:** *The act of taking money out of the bank. Also, the sum of money that is taken out.*

**FEE:** *A charge fixed by a bank for a service, such as renting a safe deposit box, buying a traveler's check, or handling an account.*

## Preparing for the First Field Trip to the Bank

At this point, you will have made friends with a specific official at your bank, if possible, explained to your child what a bank is and how it works, and introduced the basic concepts that you will be using at the bank.

The next step is to speak with your banking official and make an appointment for you and your child to visit the bank. This may take some maneuvering since banks are open the hours your child is in school. Most banks, however, are open a few hours later at least one afternoon, or on Saturday mornings, so check and see what your bank's hours are.

Explain to the bank official that you are working with your child in many areas of money management, and the time has come to open a savings account for the youngster. This will be your main order of business on your first trip with the child, but not your only goal. You also want your young one to see the bank, and witness first-hand how it operates.

Ask the bank official if it is possible for the youngster to see the vault and the safe-deposit box area. It is illegal to show the public the teller's windows on the teller's side, so just ask for a short explanation. A quick tour should only take a few minutes, and it will make an impression the child will never forget.

> **IMPORTANT NOTE:** *Be sure to bring proper identification for both you and your child. You will need this to open a bank account of any kind.*
>
> *Appropriate identification can be a passport, driver's license, or an original birth certificate.*
>
> *You will also need your child's Social Security number. (If you don't have one for the child, check with your local post office or Social Security office for the form needed to obtain one.)*

## The Grand Tour

If someone from the bank can't give you and your child a tour, you will be the chief tour guide through the bank. Here are some pointers for making your child's tour valuable:

### 1. START OUTSIDE.

Most banks will have double doors into the bank. This is because there is generally a lot of traffic in and out of a bank, and double doors help to cut the draft. More importantly, it is a security factor—double doors take longer to go through, thus slowing down anyone trying to make too quick an exit.

There will be a night depository opening in an outside wall of the bank. This looks something like a mail box opening and is used to accept deposits of money after hours when the bank is closed. A night depository is only for smaller retail customers like shops and restaurants that take in large sums of cash each day and need to deposit it for safe keeping after banking hours. (Larger retail stores and other major money handlers usually use an independent money courier, like Brink's, to transfer money to and from the bank.) As an individual customer, you and your child would not use the night depository.

Two more things you might want to point out to your youngster (if the bank has them) are the drive-through teller's window(s) and the automated teller machine (ATM). I will go into more explanation about ATMs later.

### 2. INTRODUCE YOUR CHILD TO THE GUARD.

Unless the guard is otherwise engaged, you might take your child up to him or her and introduce yourselves. Explain that this is the youngster's first trip to the bank, and that you will be visiting regularly. He or she may offer to explain security's role at the bank. If not, don't press it. It may be a rule of the bank's not to discuss these subjects.

The subject of bank robberies is bound to come up. Tread gently here. Banks don't like loud talk or jokes about bank robberies any more than airlines like discussions about bombs or hijackers. It's best to discuss this *before* you get to the bank, and try to emphasize discretion on your child's part.

### 3. POINT OUT THE DIFFERENT AREAS OF THE BANK.

Show your child the tellers, loans, safe-deposit boxes, bank offices, customer service area.

### 4. ATTEND TO BUSINESS.

Ask to speak with your Marcus Welby or bank official about opening a new account. If your child is old enough, have her explain to the bank official what she wants to do (open a savings account). Let the youngster ask, and answer, as many questions as she is able. She will remember and benefit from the experience more if she is a participant than an observer.

## 5. POINT OUT THE SIGNS INDICATING THE INTEREST PAID FOR CD'S AND OTHER TYPES OF ACCOUNTS.

Before you leave the bank, show your child the posters and signs that indicate the various interest rates and financial products the bank offers.

---

### BANK WORKSHEET

---

Here is a list of questions the child might want to ask a bank about a savings account:

1.  How much money do I need to open a savings account?
    ANSWER _____
2.  What are your bank's monthly fees or charges for a savings account?
    ANSWER _____
3.  How do I pay the fees I owe?
    ANSWER _____
4.  What is the minimum amount of money I need each time I make a deposit?
    ANSWER _____
5.  Can I withdraw money at any time?
    ANSWER _____
6.  How do I know how much money I have in the account?
    ANSWER _____
7.  How much interest does the bank pay, and when do I get the interest?
    ANSWER _____
8.  What happens if I lose the passbook or the dog eats it?
    ANSWER _____

---

**ANSWERS**

1. Each bank has its own minimum. Check with your bank to see what the balance must be so that there is no service charge. (You don't want your five-year-old's $50 savings eaten away in six months because the bank has a $7 per month service charge on accounts under $100.) Many banks will allow you to combine balances, yours with the child's, so the smaller account is not charged a monthly fee. If not, you may want to put enough of your money in the child's account to raise the balance so no fee is charged.
2. Fees vary, so check with your bank.
3. Most banks automatically deduct fees each month.
4. Usually it must be at least $1.
5. Anytime during banking hours. If you withdraw *all* the money, the bank automatically closes the account.
6. The passbook will show a running balance, or total, of your account, plus a list of the dates of your deposits and withdrawals. With a statement savings account, the child will receive a monthly or quarterly statement in the mail that describes all activity on the account. Also, you can telephone or go to the bank and ask for your balance.
7. Most banks pay interest quarterly, or four times a year, and you get the money at that time. Even if you take part of your savings out, or close the account, the quarterly interest that has been paid is still yours to keep.
8. When you present proper identification, the bank will replace the passbook.

## *How to Open a Checking Account*

A checking account is the second most popular account at a bank. It is a little more complicated to open and understand than a savings account, and it requires a great deal more responsibility.

Most children would not have a need for a checking account until they are in their teens and they are paying bills or making large purchases, but there are exceptions. When I created The First Children's Bank (located inside the F. A. O. Schwarz toy store) in 1988, I offered checking accounts to children who were six years old and above. (By New York State law, a youngster had to be old enough to sign his or her name to legally open their own account.)

Checking accounts at The First Children's Bank required the signature of both the parent and the child on checks so that the adult could monitor the account as the youngster was learning. Surprisingly, it was very popular among *employed* children who received real paychecks.

Many of The First Children's Bank customers in New York City were actors, models, or performers of some sort. Each week, many would come in with their paycheck (some were for several thousands of dollars) and deposit it. Much of the money went into savings accounts or in our College CDs, a special CD we offered to save for college, but checking accounts were most popular.

While your young nonteenager may not need to open a checking account just yet, it is valuable for him to begin to understand what it is and how it works because it is an important activity in banking.

Let's start with a child's definition of a check:

**CHECK:** *A written order to a bank to pay a specified amount of money to a specified person or company from money on deposit with the bank.*

A checking account is one that lets you keep your money in a safe place and still use it anytime you need it. Instead of carrying cash to pay for everything you buy, you can write a check.

When you open a checking account, you will get checks

from the bank to use with your name, address, and telephone number (optional) printed on the checks. Then you are ready to start writing checks.

A check tells your bank how much you want them to pay from your bank account to someone else. Show your youngster what a check looks like (see illustration or use one of your checks). Point out each of the blank spaces and what information must be filled in by the check owner (you) before the check can be processed.

Here are step-by-step instructions on how to write a check:

## HOW TO WRITE A CHECK

1. *Always Use an Ink Pen to Write on a Check.* It is important to only use ink so that the information cannot be erased or changed. If you make a mistake, do not write over it. Instead, write in big letters across the check the word "VOID."

DOLLAR BILL
GREEN STREETS COMMON
USA

0001

Oct. 31 1993
TODAY'S DATE

PAY TO THE ORDER OF  SWEET SUE'S  $ 34.51
WHO GETS THE MONEY?    HOW MUCH MONEY, IN NUMBERS?

Thirty four dollars 51/100  DOLLARS
HOW MUCH MONEY, IN WORDS?

Children's Financial Network, inc.

Penny Bright
SIGN YOUR NAME HERE

121485020383    NOT NEGOTIABLE

This means the check is no good and cannot be used by any-body. Rip it up and start again with a new check. Be sure to note this void in your check register.

2. *Fill in the Date.* Fill in the month, day, and year that you are writing the check.

3. *Write the Name of the Company or Person to Get the Money.* All checks say: "Pay to the order of." You must fill in the proper name of the person or company that you want to get the money. You must use the person or company's full name; "Grandma" or "Billy" won't do!

4. *Write the Amount of the Check in Numbers.* In this box, you fill in the dollars and cents of the check.

5. *Write Out in Words the Dollar Amount.* As a precaution to verify that you mean $40 and not $4,000 on the check (for example), this space is provided to write in words the dollar amount of the check. The cents are written in numbers.

6. *Sign Your Name.* The final step is for you to sign the check in the space at the bottom (no printing). This signature must match the signature card at the bank that you fill out when the check-ing account is opened.

---

Banks don't check every signature on every check, but some do periodic random verification of signatures. Explain to your child that it is illegal for anyone but the owner of the checking account to use the checks.

If you lose your checks or they are stolen, you must call the bank and report the loss immediately. The bank will place a stop payment on the checks so no money will be taken (debited) from your account. If a forged check is cashed, the bank is responsible for the money, not you.

By law, you must always have enough money in your account to pay the amount on the check. Another advan-tage of checks is that they give you proof that you have paid a bill.

Every time you write a check, you must keep a record of the check. Some checks have a part just for this called *check stubs*. Other checkbooks have a separate section called a *register* where you write down the information, and there are checks that create a carbon copy of each check you write. By keeping track of how much money you have spent with checks, you will always know how much money you have in the bank.

Once every month, the bank sends a *statement* to each customer. It tells how much money has been spent or deposited that month, and how much is still in the bank.

*Balancing a checkbook* means that you make sure that what the bank statement says you have spent or deposited is the same amount that your own records show. This is simple to do. Just follow these steps:

## HOW TO BALANCE A CHECKBOOK

(Before you begin, be sure to note any bank fees in your own record and to deduct them from your balance.)

1. Write down the closing balance, which the bank has listed.
2. Add to this amount any deposits you made that the bank has not yet recorded.
3. Subtract from this new total the amounts of any checks written or withdrawals made that did not appear on your bank statement.
4. Compare the end figure with the balance in your own record. The two numbers should be the same, and this is the amount of money you actually have in your checking account.

As I said earlier, it is illegal to write a check if you don't have enough money in the bank to cover your check. But if it is an accident, the check *bounces*—which means the money is not paid and the unpaid check is returned to the person or company you gave the check to. You will be asked to give the company cash or another check.

If you give them a check, you have to remember that it will bounce again if you don't put more money in the bank first. Usually your bank will charge you a fee for writing a bad check and often the person or company that you gave the bad check to will charge you a fee as well.

Writing a check with insufficient funds in the account is a criminal offense. People who write bad checks can be prosecuted and, if found guilty, can be sent to jail.

Checks have become the most common medium of exchange in America and throughout most of the industrialized world. People write checks more often than they use cash. In many ways, checks have replaced paper money and coins. Today there are approximately 125 million checking accounts in America.

Checks aren't necessarily better, but in many ways they are easier. (Almost 80 percent of all sales in the country are made by means of payment other than cash.) You can send checks through the mail to pay bills instead of having to carry the exact amount of cash to pay the companies you owe money to. Checks are safer to carry than money because a blank check has no value.

Here are some additional financial products and services that are found in a bank:

**MONEY ORDER.**

You can buy a money order from a post office or bank. You don't need a bank account to buy one, and you will have a receipt to verify that you purchased the order. It can be cashed anywhere in the country. A money order states to whom you want the money to be paid. The person cashing the money order must show identification when he or she cashes it.

## TRAVELER'S CHECKS.

This is a safer way of carrying large amounts of money with you when you travel and need to have cash, or a cash equivalency. It is safe because if traveler's checks are lost or stolen, they can be replaced, often within twenty-four hours, wherever you are. They can be used at the many businesses, hotels, and restaurants that won't take a personal check or certain credit cards.

You can buy traveler's checks at banks, and if you wish you may buy the checks in a foreign currency. Usually the bank charges 1 percent of the total amount of the checks as a service charge.

## BANK CARD.

A bank card is a small plastic card that lets you use your bank's *automated teller machine (ATM)*, also called a *cash machine*. The ATM card has a secret number (called a *personal identification number*, or *PIN*) encoded electronically on it. You can do nearly all your banking electronically from an ATM machine, twenty-four hours a day. You can deposit money, transfer money from one account to another within the same bank, withdraw money, and even pay some bills.

I might add here that electronic banking is definitely the wave of the future. In fact, many banks are offering the same services that an ATM offers through a touch-tone phone or your home computer.

Another note: you can do your banking by mail if you wish. It takes a little longer to register a deposit because of the mail, but if the convenience is important to you, check with your bank to see how to do it.

## SAFE-DEPOSIT BOX.

This is a secure metal box, usually about half the size of a shoe box, that is kept in the bank's vault and can be rented by a bank customer. People keep important papers in them, like stocks, bonds, wills, and insurance policies, and maybe some small valuable items like jewelry.

**CREDIT CARDS.**

Another very important financial product is a bank credit card, like Visa or MasterCard. This is really for older teenage children and I will describe these and all credit cards later in the chapter on teens.

# 6 How to Use the World as Your Financial Classroom

This is a crucial chapter so I've divided it into two sections. To start, I will show you how to work with your child to utilize the time and experiences you already share. Then I'll talk about consumerism: how to be a better consumer and the very important concept of *relative value*, which enables a consumer of any age to make better buying decisions.

First, though, let me reassure you about one thing. Most parents already feel pressure to instruct their children on a range of subjects. (Goodness knows potty-training alone takes a lot out of you!) You may be asking yourself, "How can I, the over-burdened parent, have the time or energy to approach one more topic?"

When it comes to the subject of money, you can. It's easier than you might think, and in this chapter I'm going to show you how. You will not have to formulate lesson plans or run out and get a degree in finance. I will offer several suggestions and ideas, as well as the tools (such as the correct financial language to use with your child and wonderful, go-anywhere games) to teach the basics of money management to your youngster.

Your "classroom" will be anywhere you want it to be, and at a time you choose—while you're fixing dinner, reading the newspaper, doing the weekly grocery shopping, or on a car trip. Not only will you be passing on money management tips, you might even improve the quality of the time you spend with your youngster.

## How Parents (Inadvertently) Teach Children

Think about how you currently work with your offspring. Most parents teach their children in two different ways—one is unconsciously (by example) and the other is very deliberately when something happens that reminds them to speak to the child, which I call environmental teaching.

A parent unconsciously imparts knowledge simply because he or she and the spouse are the child's principal role models. Your youngster watches what you do very carefully. The kid studies your moves and your actions as well as your language, and then mimicks much of your behavior—even the way you spend money!

You did the same thing with your parents. For instance, do you prefer to buy two weeks of groceries all at once or do you run in and pick up just what you need every day or so? Is that how your parent grocery-shopped? Then chances are, that's how your offspring will shop too.

Here's another example: do you wait until the needle on your gas gauge is on (or past) empty, or do you try and fill up at the half-empty mark? Do you buy a new car every year or two, or do you wait until the automobile is severely disabled before looking at new ones?

These are all examples of consumer behavior, and by definition, that involves the use of money. Some might argue that one method is more efficient than another, but generally speaking, you are the judge of that. Just keep in mind that your youngster will most likely pick up this behavior.

## Environmental Training

The second way you impart knowledge to your youngster, as I said, is very conscious. It is a moment in everyday life where you stop and explain or instruct your child in some manner. I call it environmental training, because usually it is something in the everyday environment, special surroundings, or circumstances that triggers you to conduct a quick on-the-spot lesson.

For instance, you probably are reminded to bring up and discuss the subject of proper table manners during dinner when you notice that your darling is chattering away *and* chewing at the same time. Or you explain the basics of baking a cake or filling the lawn mower with gasoline as you're doing it with your child standing over you.

## Your Go-Anywhere Financial Classroom

Real life triggers the lessons you want to teach your child, and since you are probably handling money regularly in front of your child, stop and take two minutes to explain what you're doing. It will last a lifetime.

A friend told me the story of driving across country with his three young children to visit the grandparents at Christmastime. During the trip, the four-year-old son was always the last one out of the restaurant after each meal.

Finally, when they were almost home, the annoyed father asked his young son why he straggled behind. The youngster reached into his pocket, pulled out a handful of change and said, "Because I have to go back and check the table to see that you haven't accidentally left your money behind."

After the waves of anger and humiliation left my very proper friend (he was tempted but refrained from driving back to each restaurant to make reparations), the father realized that, to a child, the routine act of leaving money on the table would appear to be extreme carelessness.

I had a similar experience with my son, Rhett, when he was very young and we were window shopping at the magical F. A. O. Schwarz toy store in New York City. The youngster (having inherited very expensive tastes from his parent) eyed a magnificent child-sized red Ferrari with an adult-sized price tag.

Rhett was enthralled and wanted the car immediately. When I explained that I did not have the money for such an expensive toy, he suggested I use "one of those magic plastic cards" in the place of money! By watching me, he understood that a credit card was a substitute for money—but not that it was only a temporary replacement.

*Children are not clairvoyant.* Leaving money on the table as a tip for the waitress can easily appear careless to a young child, and a check or credit card gives the illusion of being able to magically escape from actually having to spend real money. Your kids won't understand what you're doing with money unless you explain it to them—so don't keep it a secret!

The idea is to take a moment to explain to your child what you are doing with your money, checks, or credit cards as you are doing it. The next time you're in a restaurant or waiting in line for gas, make that moment your "classroom lesson" for the day. It will be a lot easier for you, the teacher, and a more powerful illustration to the student.

With the exception of what you show your youngster at the bank (Chapters 5 and 8), most of your classroom will be in retail outlets—the stores where you go to buy a screwdriver or bread or gasoline. This is where your money changes hands most frequently and most visibly to your child.

Later in this chapter, I will describe specific games and exercises for you and your youngster to do while you're in your classroom/store.

Before I get into those activities, though, I want to go back one step to talk a bit about consumerism—a significant piece of money management—and how to be a good, prudent consumer whether you are age six or sixty.

## What Is a Consumer?

Teaching your youngster how to spend money is not going to be the hardest task you face as a parent; teaching them how to spend money carefully and with intelligence, though, will be a challenge.

If a child is old enough to spend money in a store alone, then he or she is old enough to think about the decision-making process that goes into spending money. You, the parent, can help the youngster learn how to spend money carefully and wisely so that they are satisfied with the decisions they have made.

Our overall goal here is to raise your child's financial IQ to its highest level. What that means is showing your youngster how to be intelligent in his or her dealings with money, both in saving *and* in spending it.

Start by explaining that spending money is usually a conscious, deliberate decision that the spender makes. There are exceptions, like taxes and such, but you pretty much choose when and where you will spend money just as you pick what you will eat or not eat. The responsibility of making the right choice is on the spender (and the eater).

It also is valuable to point out to your child that as Americans, we are the most blessed in terms of the many choices and ways we have to spend money. There is no other marketplace in the world with the range and variety of products that the United States has to offer. Whether it is the flavor of ice cream, the color of automobile, or the type of videotape from the movie store, we have dozens and dozens of choices to make about the things we buy.

This great blessing has one down side. The "consumer heaven" that we enjoy in this country also presents us with tremendous temptations to spend money we either don't have, or have planned to spend another way. What does the wise money manager do to keep from being derailed from his long-term financial goals?

He or she has a budget! A budget will ease the decision-making process of how to spend money, because a budget, like a road map, lays out in advance how you will choose to spend money (Chapter 4). With or without a budget, we will show you how to help your child become a savvy consumer.

Let's address the spending part of money management for a minute. When you buy something for yourself or your family, you immediately become a *consumer*. You've been a consumer for many years, and if your child is much older than two and a half, he or she is probably a budding consumer, too.

The thing about being a consumer is that most of us, unless we are diagnosed with the very rare saver personality, seem to be born with an innate ability to spend money, or consume, very easily. It requires little, if any, actual training or education—and it's lots and lots of fun!

Here's Webster's definition of consumer: "a person who buys goods or services for his own needs" (as opposed to a retailer or manufacturer who buys things for resale). Here's my definition of a smart consumer: someone who buys intelligently and stays within the assigned budget.

There is a difference between being a good buyer and being a good consumer. For example, my lovely friend Judy was very excited about finding, in the far corner of a neighborhood discount store, bottles of $100 champagne on sale for $66. She bought a case of the champagne, which would have been just fine except for the fact that Judy had been out of work for six months and champagne was not what she needed most under the circumstances. The champagne was a good buy; whether Judy was being a good consumer is questionable.

A careless or undisciplined consumer gets into financial difficulty very quickly *no matter how much money they have.* Unless you are a compulsive gambler or recklessly play the stock market (which are different types of problems), being a bad consumer is a major reason most people fail with money.

Perhaps the single most dramatic area where you can raise your child's financial IQ is by teaching him to become a good consumer. It requires self-discipline, knowledge, judgment, and often a little investigative work, but it is an attainable goal and crucial to anyone's success as a money manager.

## How to Teach Your Child the Principles of Smart Spending

How do you begin to make a concerted effort to purchase only what you need and really want, and ignore the enormous pressures to buy what you don't need and don't really want? How do you stick to that budget? I'll detail some of the rules to follow, and the games and exercises that will make staying on a budget a lot more fun for you and your child.

First, start by explaining to your little one what "good" spending and "bad" spending are. Good spending might be when you use money to buy something you really need, like notebook paper for school. Bad spending is when you use all the money you have in your wallet to buy candy. Think of your own examples of good and bad spending that will be meaningful to your child.

Next, explain that your goal, and the child's, is to learn how to be a good spender, or consumer. Here's a younger child's definition:

**GOOD CONSUMER:** *A person who spends money wisely.*

Sounds pretty simple, eh? So is the formula for becoming a good consumer. It requires equal parts of doing some research and planning, or "homework" as I like to call it, before you even walk into a store, and then a healthy dose of self-discipline once you're there.

RESEARCH + PLAN (BUDGET) + DISCIPLINE = GOOD CONSUMER

Let me expand a bit on this formula because I think it cuts to the heart of being a wise consumer and a savvy financial manager.

Planning what you want to buy (before you're in the store and tempted to do otherwise) is the key to successful financial management. When you formulate such a plan, it's called a budget, and I've devoted a whole chapter in this book to how to do that (Chapter 4).

Before you lay out an entire annual budget for you or your child, keep in mind that planning what you want to buy is as important for the little ways you want to use your money (like a quick trip to the grocery) as the big, long-range things (like buying a bicycle or a car).

Most people do the greatest amount of damage to their budgets through spur-of-the-moment impulse buying. *Plan* what you want to get before you leave the house.

Research means gathering all the pertinent information about what you intend to purchase *before* you walk into a store. If I had to go out and buy a CD player today, I honestly wouldn't know if it should cost $50 or $500, and heaven help me if I relied on a suave, persuasive salesperson to guide me.

Chances are that, as a parent, you already have your "degree" in consumer research: you listen to and read the advertisements for products (and sales); you check with a neighbor to see where he got a good deal on a weedeater before you buy one; you take the tip when a friend mentions where she stocked up on sale-priced toilet paper; you clip only the coupons in the newspaper for the items you regularly buy anyway before heading to the market. Those are all good consumer research techniques.

I have a system for doing this that I call my M.E.S.S. program and I encourage you, and your child, to make a M.E.S.S.!

Here is what the M.E.S.S. system is and how it works:

---

## THE M.E.S.S. SYSTEM

---

**M** — *Make a List.* Making a shopping list is vital because it forces you to decide *in advance* what you really need, what you don't need, and what you don't need to buy this week before you're in the high-pressure environment of a store. It also reminds you to take measurements or inventory your supply before you leave the house.

**E** — *Evaluate What Are Truly Basic Necessities and What Are Not in Your Household.* The necessities are the basic supplies you and your family use regularly and need to have stocked at all times. I make three separate lists for this: Toiletries, Pantry, and House.

When in doubt, I ask myself, "Can I live without this?" If the object is toilet paper, the answer is obviously no. If it's sweets for the living room candy dish, the response is yes.

The list could look something like this:

### The Basic Necessities List

| *Toiletries* | *Kitchen* | *House* |
|---|---|---|
| Shampoo | Flour | Dishwashing soap |
| Deodorant | Sugar | Garbage bags |
| Bar soap | Coffee | Vacuum cleaner bags |

Some rainy afternoon, why don't you sit down with your child and form your own basic necessities list? It's fun! My children and I did this on a long plane ride recently, and—with the help of our fellow passengers—we got into some passionate discussions over what was a basic item and what wasn't (Cap'n Crunch cereal was, grape jelly was not).

Once you've established what is essential and what is not, your in-store shopping decisions are much easier to make. Now, more about making a M.E.S.S.:

**S —** *Shop the Ads*. As suspicious as we've all become of most advertising, it still is the best vehicle for communicating what products and services are available at what price. Particularly for big-ticket items like a mattress or refrigerator, ads can alert you to where the best buys are. Also, don't forget TV ads and weekly newspapers.

For me, this is the most exciting aspect of the shopping game. I view it as an intellectual challenge to hunt for the lowest price, and I have fun finding it!

**S —** *Stick to the Agenda*. It is soooooooo easy to get distracted and impulse-buy your way through a store. Don't. Stick to your list! Be prudent about tossing (or letting young ones toss) additional items into the cart as you roll down the aisle.

**CONSUMER TIP:** *The really good buys are usually well displayed at the end of aisles, not buried mid-aisle. So to save further temptation, I suggest hitting the departments you need for the things on your list, take a quick glance down the main aisle, then run to the checkout counter!*

In talking to people on my weekly television show, *Money Talk!*, I've seen that everybody has trouble from time to time with controlling the urge to spend money. My viewers have often asked me questions on this subject, and I'll pass these tips on to you and your young consumer protégés:

### THE OUT-OF-SIGHT PLAN.

So many people have said to me, "If the money is in my wallet, it's gone. I find a way to spend it." Well, now that's an easy problem to fix, isn't it? These days, it is not intelligent to carry large sums of money around anyway, so if you're doing that, figure out another way.

My wonderful assistant, Suzy, had a mild version of this problem and fixed it. She works and gets paid in one state (New York), and lives and banks in a neighboring state (Connecticut). Each payday, Suzy cashed her paycheck where she worked so that she could deposit the cash in her bank and begin writing checks immediately. (At her bank, an out-of-state check takes up to ten days to clear.)

The problem was that between the time Suzy cashed her check on Thursday, and deposited it in her bank on Saturday, a large chunk somehow mysteriously "evaporated" from her wallet. Her solution? Upon cashing her check, Suzy took out just enough to cover her expenses, plus $20 for emergencies, and then put the rest in a sealed envelope someplace other than her wallet. This gave her the peace of mind that she had cash for expenses, but not extra money available to tempt her.

A friend who is a psychiatrist and wonderful at explaining human behavior reminds me that "money is power," or rather it can give you the feeling of power. "I can do, or buy, anything I want" is the subconscious thinking. Yet the act of carrying around large sums of money, particularly for the spender personality, is like carrying a loaded gun. It's bound to get one into trouble.

**LEAVE-THE-CREDIT-CARDS-AT-HOME PLAN.**

Same as for the carrying-too-much-cash problem. If it's not with you, you can look, but you can't spend.

These suggestions may fall more under the heading of "Games We Play with Ourselves" than savvy money management techniques. What works for you, and your youngster, is the important thing.

## The Concept of Relative Value and Its Importance

Relative value is one of the most important educational concepts that I will address in this book. It is the cornerstone of teaching responsible financial management, and the basis for making intelligent decisions about money.

*Relative value* means what one thing costs in relation to what you personally have to do to pay for it. Relative value is the "real" cost of something, and it can make your and your child's purchasing decisions much clearer.

For example, to take your family of four on vacation for a week to DisneyWorld, it may cost you a total of $4,000. Now think of the cost of that vacation in a different way. Did you have to work one week to earn the money, or eight weeks? You may have spent $4,000 in money, but in terms of relative value, that vacation cost you X number of weeks of sweat.

Now, put that figure in terms your child can understand. How long would a kid have to work and save all of an allowance to pay for the family vacation? An eight-year-old with a weekly allowance of $8 would have to save the entire allowance for a total of nine years, six months, and one week to pay for the DisneyWorld vacation. Impressive figures, eh? Relative value puts a whole new perspective on the *real* cost of things.

Here is a child's definition:

RELATIVE VALUE: *The real price of something in terms of what it will cost you in work and time.*

Relative value redefines what something costs and puts it in terms of what the individual has to do to earn it. Clearly, as we have seen with the DisneyWorld vacation, it differs from one person to another. The baseball mitt that your twelve-year-old wants to buy is going to have a different relative value for your six-year-old.

You can explain relative value in other ways. That $4,000 vacation, for instance, also might represent one half of the cost of a new car. Therefore:

New Car $= 2 \times$ DisneyWorld vacation

or

20 New Cars $= 1$ New House

For our purposes, I suggest that you stick to what an item costs in terms of time and sweat when explaining relative value. It will make a stronger impression on your youngster.

When your child understands the relative value of a product or service, then he can begin to make an informed decision on whether it is a wise use of his money. And after all, when it comes to talent, beauty, intelligence, or money, it's not how much you have, but how well you use it!

## How to Use Relative Value as a Teaching Tool

Now that you and your child are comfortable with the concept of relative value, think about ways you can use this idea as you work with your child and money.

Actually, there are two ways you can talk about relative value. One way, as we just discussed, is in terms of time and how long a period of time it takes a child to save for something. For example, it will take your young one two weeks to save his $4-a-week allowance to buy a $5.95 fire truck. In other words, he has to wait two weeks and not buy anything else to earn this toy.

Another way to impress your youngster with the relative value of an item is in terms of labor. How many lawns will Johnny or Jenny have to cut to pay for a new Nintendo game? Five? Ten? The idea of cutting ten lawns to earn the money for a computer game helps a kid decide—and almost instantly—whether he or she really wants the item. This kind of relative value shopping conveys the real price of the toy by putting the cost into a framework the child can understand.

Use the concept of relative value to help your youngster set his or her priorities, and to understand yours. For the older kid who is dying for a $70 pair of Reeboks, it might be valuable to point out that to the child those shoes may represent X number of weeks of allowance or X number of lawns to cut, but to you, $70 represents what it costs to pay the electric bill for one month.

Another tack you may want to take on occasion with your child is how long you, the parent, have to work to earn the $70 for the Reeboks. Is it a half day? A whole day? This would indicate to the child that a $70 pair of shoes is expensive, even to an adult.

Be creative and keep explaining relative value in different ways to children. Your goal is to encourage your youngster to get into the habit of asking, "What will this cost me in time or labor?" Eventually, it will begin to sink in.

To help or reinforce the concept of relative value, I've created the following game. It is similar to the popular TV game *The Price Is Right*. It can be played at home and with several people.

## THE RELATIVE VALUE GAME

**GOAL:**

To teach children the concept of relative value.

**TOOLS:**

Magazine or newspaper pictures of products, pencil and paper for each contestant, and a moderator/judge (usually the parent).

**RULES:**

The moderator holds up the picture of a specific product and each contestant guesses the price *in terms of relative value,* i.e., how many weeks of allowance the product costs, or how many extra jobs (baby-sitting, cutting lawns, etc.) would go into paying for the item.

Example: A woman's pair of jeans.

**HOW TO WIN:**

After all the guesses are in, the youngster who comes closest without going over the actual cost wins.

**MISSION:**

The child must correctly guess the dollar amount as translated into his or her weeks of allowance or number of jobs. For example, the youngster may guess that the jeans cost her four weeks of allowance or seven hours of baby-sitting time.

---

Once you and your child are comfortable and conversant with the concept of relative value, continue on with the next idea, which is "comparative value."

## *How to Explain and Use the Concept of Comparative Shopping*

The relative value of an item is addressed once you've chosen a product or service that you are considering buying. Before you get to that point, though, you should have done some *comparative shopping* (remember our M.E.S.S. system?) to get an idea of what things cost.

Ideally, particularly with big-ticket items, you have read the consumer magazines and checked the ads to see what the choices and prices are. Then you go to the store and look at the item, compare it to a less expensive and more expensive item, and make the buying decision—or not.

More often, however, I find myself standing in the house-hold cleaning products aisle looking for something I don't use frequently, like silver polish. "Which one should I buy?" I ask myself. This is when I use my comparative shopping skills.

I am looking at similar, but not identical, products. I pick up a brand that is familiar; I look at the price and the number of ounces. I pick up another brand, or perhaps the generic silver polish cleaner, and see what it says. Then I make a decision on which one is best to buy.

You know what I'm doing, and probably do it all the time as you shop. Now, how do you explain this decision-making process to a young one? Let's start with a definition:

**COMPARATIVE SHOPPING:** *To note the likenesses and differences between two or more things that you are considering buying.*

Comparative shopping is best done "in the field," so try this exercise with your four- to twelve-year-old at the grocery store:

## THE COMPARATIVE SHOPPING GAME

**GOAL:**
To teach the basics of budgeting and comparative shopping.
**TOOLS:**
Pad, pencil, and calculator.

**RULES:**

At the beginning of each aisle in the store, the parent assigns the child an item (or items for older kids) and a budget.

Example: paper products aisle.

Item: two rolls of paper towels.

Budget: $3.

**HOW TO WIN:**

After all the shopping is completed, if the youngster comes under the alotted budget, he or she gets to keep the savings. The child with the most money saved wins the game.

**MISSION:**

The child must find the item(s) the parent wants without spending more than the budget allows.

---

As you begin to play this game in the grocery store with your youngster, it is a good time to show him generic brand products. Explain why you believe some generic products are better or worse than others. Don't forget to look at the ingredients on the labels—this may help your case!

## How to Use the World as Your Classroom

Okay, you and your child have made a M.E.S.S., discussed the concept of relative value, and done a little comparative shopping. The next order of business is to arrange another field trip so that you can practice more of these ideas in the real world.

At my house, this is called running errands and it usually takes place on Saturday mornings.

Most of us who are working parents do not have the services of a full-time butler and housekeeper, so we devote our Saturdays to doing household chores and running errands. Errands are those little stops all over town to pick up the dry cleaning, leave film to be developed, fill prescriptions, pick up a new screwdriver at the hardware store, etc., etc., etc.

Running errands is an excellent way to spend time with your youngster while you tootle around town. If you have more than one child, you may find that taking a different youngster with you each week is a way of making each child feel special.

Again, whatever chore or errand is on your route, take a minute to explain what it is you're doing to the youngster.

Here are several in-store games. These games work best in a large supermarket, but are adaptable to the drug store, hardware store, and other retail outlets. They are easy, fun, and can be used with one child or several. All the games are designed to teach and reinforce good consumer buying habits:

## THE COUPON GAME
### (A good game for younger children)

**GOAL:**
To teach a child how to use coupons effectively.

**TOOLS:**
Coupons clipped from newspapers or magazines.

**RULES:**
Coupons must only be for items on your Basic Necessities List (see page 93) or on your shopping list.

**HOW TO WIN:**
For every item chosen by the child that the cashier accepts with a coupon, the youngster gets to keep the money saved from the coupon.

**MISSION:**
To show your youngster how coupons work. Usually there are specific product sizes that must be chosen, there are expiration dates, and only limited quantities can be purchased.

Here is another game for youngsters just learning how to read:

## THE LABEL-CHECKING GAME

**GOAL:**
To teach the child what to look for on the label (price, size, calories, ingredients, and so forth).

**TOOLS:**
A grocery store.

**RULES:**
Assign the child the task of finding a product with your specifics, e.g., single-serving size, low-salt product, whatever it may be. Send the child a couple of aisles ahead of you and the shopping cart.

Example: The child must find a breakfast cereal where the first ingredient is *not* sugar. Or find a fragrance-free toilet paper in the color blue.

**MISSION:**
The child must find the correct item before you and the shopping cart reach the aisle. Then, without knowing what the child picked, you choose the item and compare it with what the youngster picked.

**HOW TO WIN:**
If the item your child picked is the same as your choice, or if it is a better buy, the youngster wins and gets to pick one item in the store as a prize.

Remember, when you and your child are shopping together, try to talk about the reasons behind your consumer behavior in the store. For instance, do you keep a running total of what you're buying, or do you add it up in your head at the checkout counter?

You also might want to explain why stores do certain

things to inspire more buying. For instance, point out to your youngster the magazine and candy racks that are usually located at the checkout counter. Why are they there? So the store can catch impulse buyers as they wait in line.

If your grocery store cashier uses an electronic scanner to register the price, show your youngster how this works. Notice that the cashier might run one item that you are purchasing several of over the electronic eye several times, or they might punch in the quantity manually. Explain why the cashier does this.

Also, show the child how to keep an eye on the monitor, especially for items that are on sale. The prices on the item might not be properly recorded on the register.

Here are some other classrooms besides the supermarket:

### GAS STATION.

Many people fluctuate between using the full-service and self-serve lanes at the gas station. You may choose full service so that you can get the oil or tires checked, or, if you're like me, because you're wearing white shoes that day and don't want to spill gasoline on them!

Take a minute to explain the difference in price versus service at the gas station, and why you use both for different reasons.

Another point at the pumps: sometimes one station will sell gas several cents below the station across the street. Show your youngster where the prices are posted, and how to shop for the best price.

Also, your regular gas station may charge less if you pay with cash rather than with a credit card. Discuss with your youngster why it costs a business more to use credit cards.

### DRY CLEANER.

Like the gas station, a dry cleaner offers a service that you may choose to use or not.

I personally have adopted my good friend Bonnie's system of deciding which services are worth utilizing and which aren't. Bonnie is a retail consultant, and her clients pay her $50 an hour for her professional sevices. She figures her personal time also is worth about that, so when she has to decide whether to wash and iron her husband's five business shirts each week, she calculates what it will cost in terms of her valuable time as opposed to using the services of a dry cleaner. Bonnie sees the dry cleaner's $1.99 a shirt as a bargain.

Explain to your youngster that while you might not want to clean a wool coat yourself, you might *choose* to send a silk blouse to the cleaners rather than wash it yourself, if you were pressed (no pun intended) for time. The same might be true for things like a shoe shine, a shave at the barber's, a manicure or a shampoo and set at the beauty parlor.

## How You Instill Your Personal Values through Consumerism

So you think that personal values are only taught in church or synagogue, right? Think again. There are a few buying decisions that you make that may supersede conventional wisdom and, believe it or not, this is allowed.

Usually, these decisions are based on your personal convictions. They can be for political or religious reasons, or out of personal loyalty. For instance, do you refuse to drive anything but an American-made car? Do you shy away from buying items made by anti-American countries? Or do you buy only General Foods products because you, or someone in your family, works for General Foods?

Whatever the reason, if it strongly influences your buying decisions over all other considerations, you may want to explain your position to your youngsters.

A good example of teaching values through the buying decisions you make is the issue of "Made in America." This is a subject that is growing in importance and, as trade barriers fall worldwide, will continue to be significant for many people.

If buying products made in the United States is important to you, discuss why with your child. The most-often cited reason is that buying foreign-made products over American-made—even when they are less expensive—hurts us in other ways down the road. Even for something as insignificant as a $7 T-shirt, buying an import can hurt or even eliminate an American manufacturer and that means fewer American jobs. Fewer American jobs means more people need the government's help, and that means more taxes.

Try not to scare young children with too much job-loss talk, but most older kids and teenagers can handle real-life economics and understand how these small decisions affect the larger community.

There are other personal-choice buying decisions that may be important to you. A frequently used one is the issue of quality. Everyone wants to buy the highest quality product available that they can afford. Sometimes quality isn't the overriding factor, however.

I'll give you an example. A good childhood friend of mine has lived in Germany with her husband and four children for many years. When she comes to visit, I always am impressed with the beautiful, well-crafted clothes she and her youngsters wear. Janet, on the other hand, is wild to go to our all-American discount chain stores where she loads up on everything.

She says that while quality is very important to her, there are some things—like children's underwear or toys—that do not have to be built to last well into the next century. "In Germany, the quality and durability of a pair of toddlers' underpants is quite remarkable, but they cost $10 apiece. I need the five-pairs-for-five-dollars variety that you can only get at Kmart!"

There is a similar argument over the issue of buying name-brand or generic products. Do you maintain your lifelong loyalty to Brand X because of their commitment to excellence, or try the less-expensive Brand Y? There are no hard-and-fast rules, but here are some suggestions on how to make this decision:

### CONSUMER MAGAZINES.

Most of us know to turn to these publications for big-ticket items like air conditioners or television sets, but did you know that these magazines also address smaller items, from deodorant to jeans? If you have a large family, a subscription to one of these magazines can save you a lot of money. (These magazines are carried in most public libraries.)

### COMPARE INGREDIENTS.

Examine Brand X's cake mix side by side with Brand Y's. Remember that ingredients are listed starting with the largest quantity. If sugar is the number one ingredient in one mix, and second or third in another, this may factor into your decision.

### TRIAL AND ERROR.

Sometimes the only way to determine if generic brand B cleans as well as or better than name brand A is to try it. Often there are trial sizes of the products for this purpose.

All of these things relate to consumer behavior and buying habits. Often, there are no right or wrong reasons for choosing one brand over another. It is simply a matter of preference. Yet whether your buying decisions are based on personal feelings or value, it merits discussing the decisions you make with your youngster.

## *How to Watch a Commercial*

Much of our consumer behavior, and therefore our buying habits, is influenced or even set by what we read, hear, and watch in the media. Advertisements and commercials are among the strongest seducers to buy, buy, buy.

While print and radio ads can be strong influences on youngsters, I will focus here on television commercials because TV makes a big impression on a young mind.

Pollsters say that children in the United States watch an average of over two and a half hours of TV a day, and within a thirty-minute program, there can be as much as thirteen minutes' worth of commercials! Much of that advertising is targeted specifically at kids because they have money of their own to spend and because they strongly influence their parents' buying habits.

Commercials try to sell children everything from cereal to toys to tennis shoes, and there is a growing sentiment among both parents and educators against advertisers and their methods of sending conscious and subconscious buying messages to kids. Some people even feel that commercials on children's programming should be banned.

My solution is a little different. I maintain that we need to teach our children about advertising, what a commercial is and what it is trying to accomplish. You can't be coerced into doing something you don't want to do if you know and understand the process.

Here is another game that I've created to focus on learning how commercials work and how they influence us:

---

## THE TV COMMERCIAL GAME

---

**GOAL:**
To teach your child how to become a savvy consumer.
**TOOLS:**
A children's show on television; a grocery store.

---

**RULES:**

Watch a TV program with your child and pay special attention to the commercials. Explain the difference between the program and the commercial.

Ask the youngster if he or she remembers the many products there are in a grocery store. Then explain that because there are so many choices, the people who make a particular soda or cereal want to convince you through their commercial to buy their product.

Have your child pick a new product to taste-test, like a soda or a cereal. Then go to the supermarket and let your child find that product. (If it is a kid's cereal, he or she will probably find it within his reach. Explain that manufacturers put the cereal there so that kids can see it.)

Buy a similar brand, and then at home conduct a taste test with other family members. Blindfold them and let them pick their favorite, the best-tasting corn flakes or cola.

**HOW TO WIN:**

If the product your child picked from the TV commercial was the choice of the family, then he wins. Remind him or her of the points the advertiser was stressing. Was it crisper? Did it have more raisins?

**MISSION:**

Make your child aware of commercials so that the youngster can't be unduly influenced, and so that he or she will learn how to be a better consumer.

# 7 How to Explain the Terrible Ts: Tipping, Taxes, Tickets, Tokens, and Tolls

This chapter is devoted to all the funny little things we adults do almost every day without thinking. Perhaps we never even consider the merit of explaining these routine activities to our increasingly financially sophisticated youngster.

You remember the terrible twos? What I will cover here are the Terrible Ts, like tipping, taxes, tolls, and tickets. I will show you how to explain these many facts of life to your young one in ways that will make them real.

Earlier in this book, I told the story about the young boy who picked up after Daddy at restaurants because he believed his father, who left change on the table as a tip for the waitress, was carelessly leaving behind his money. The moral of the story was *don't keep secrets* about money from your child. Explain what you're doing as you're doing it, because someday the youngster will need to do it too.

Since tipping is such a mysterious act to young ones, I'll start there.

## How to Explain the What and Why of Tipping

My beloved sister and I, who routinely agree on everything from ice cream to husbands, violently disagree on one single subject in life: tipping, and, in particular, how much to tip a waiter or waitress in a restaurant. We've gone for days not speaking to each other because one felt the other left too little or too much tip. Silly, eh?

There seem to be two schools of thought on tipping. Some people feel that it is supplemental income to the server's salary and therefore only a small token of appreciation for service well done is needed. (Webster's does, in fact, define "tip" as "a small present of money for some service.")

On the other hand, others recognize that for many people, not just waiters and waitresses, tips are their primary form of income and they receive little or sometimes no other salary. Therefore, their efforts need a bit more than a "token" acknowledgment.

Whichever school of thought you embrace, I think we can all agree that there are appropriate times to tip. (You may argue with your own sibling on how much that should be.)

Let's start with who most frequently gets a tip or gratuity. Here is a list of professionals that traditionally receive a tip:

---

### PROFESSIONALS WHO RECEIVE TIPS

---

Waiters/waitresses
Maitre d's
Coat check people
Beauty parlor personnel and barbers

---

Hotel employees
Airport skycaps
Delivery people
Parking valets
Taxi drivers
Newspaper boys/girls
Doormen
Porters

---

Now, here is a child's definition of tipping:

**TIPPING:** *A small amount of money you give to someone who has served you in some way.*

I will anticipate the inevitable "why?" question by adding that, historically, tipping was used as a type of reward or expression of gratitude for a service well done.

I view tipping as a part of the normal cost of living, and I figure it into my budget just as I would taxes (which I'll address later).

The best time to explain the concept of tipping to your young child (age four to eight) is as you are about to do it. For instance, does your family love to order pizza in and watch a video on Sunday nights? Great! So take a minute to explain to your child that the pizza delivery person will bring the food, collect the money, and will expect a tip.

Let the child go with you to the door, and watch you as you pay the bill and give the delivery person the tip. (You might point out that if the delivery person has driven through a raging snowstorm or gotten there in ten minutes flat, he or she may deserve a little extra compensation.)

The same thing is true if you go to a restaurant where you sit down and are served food. Take the opportunity to quietly show the child the bill and explain how you would determine the appropriate amount of tip. If the youngster is well into grade school, let her try to figure up the tip.

How much do you tip in a restaurant? Generally, most people (except my sister) take 15 to 20 percent of the total bill and make that the tip. The low end, 15 percent, is usually for basic, unexceptional service, and the high end, 20 percent, would be for very good service.

Show the child how to set criteria to grade the server. Did the waiter or waitress bring the correct order and serve it while it was hot? Was the server prompt and attentive to your needs? Setting a standard for poor, average, good, and excellent service is helpful to a kid, and shows how to make the judgment on the amount of the tip.

> **IN-RESTAURANT EXERCISE:** *According to a recent story in* The Wall Street Journal, *over 50 percent of all restaurant bills are added up incorrectly, and most errors are in favor of the restaurant. Let your child check the addition on the bill and then figure the appropriate tip.*

Now, what do you do if the waiter or waitress has undercharged you on the bill? Do you call it to his or her attention or keep quiet? Again, this is an opportunity for parents to instill their personal values in the youngster. (Keep in mind that the poor mathematician/waiter/waitress may have to pay the difference out of their own pocket if the cashier catches the mistake later.)

---

## HOW MUCH DO YOU TIP?

---

| | |
|---|---|
| Waiters/waitresses | 15 to 20% of total bill |
| Maitre d's | $5 to $10 for a good table or moving you up in the line |

| | |
|---|---|
| Coat check people | $1 per coat or item checked |
| Beauty parlor personnel and barbers | 10 to 20% of total bill |
| Hotel bellboys | $1 per bag |
| Hotel maids | $1 per day |
| Airport skycaps | $1 per bag |
| Delivery people | 10% of bill |
| Parking valets | $1 |
| Taxi drivers | 10 to 15% of the total fare |
| Newspaper boys/girls | 50 cents per week; $20 at Christmas |
| Doormen | Tip appropriately for individual jobs; $50 at Christmas |
| Porters | $5 to $10, depending on what they do |

## HOW TO FIGURE OUT THE TIP

1. First, to figure percentage, you put a decimal point in front of the number that is the percentage, except for single figures, for which you add a 0 first (for example, 20 percent is .20 and five percent is .05).
2. Then multiply that number by the amount of the bill.
3. The total, rounded off if necessary, is the correct tip.
   EXAMPLE: If you want to leave a 15% tip on a restaurant bill of $22, you multiply $22 by .15 to get $3.30.

    Learning how to figure the tip is a good game to play with a pocket calculator at the dinner table while you're waiting for your meal. Simply give your youngster a fictional total, the percentage you wish to tip, and let him or her figure the gratuity on the calculator.

Point out to the child that sometimes, particularly in expensive restaurants, the beverage or bar tab is rung separately from the meal, so be sure to look at both sides of the bill.

Also, a server may put the totaled bill on your table after the main course is served, and then add to the bill if coffee and/or dessert are ordered later. And be alert: if you ordered something and didn't get it, make sure it is subtracted from the total bill.

In New York City, people have developed an even quicker way of determining the tip. The tax on restaurant food is eight and a quarter percent, so if that figure is doubled, the tip works out to be a little over 16 percent.

## How to Explain Taxes

Often when I am lecturing about children and money, the subject of taxes comes up. I will stop and ask a child in the audience, "Do you think taxes are a good thing or a bad thing?"

Invariably, the youngster says that taxes are bad, which is a good example of how parents inadvertently convey their value system to children. In truth, taxes may be too high or too low or even allocated improperly, but they are not, in and of themselves, bad.

We adults may grumble about paying taxes, but keep in mind that they are not inherently evil. Taxes pay for many things the average American (or even a billionaire like Ross Perot) could not afford to buy on their own.

Taxes pay for things like roads and bridges, sewers, sidewalks, schools, teachers, policemen and firemen, and so forth. It's our tax dollars that help to win wars and send people to the moon. Taxes are an important and necessary cost of living in the United States.

Here is a definition of taxes for your six- to twelve-year-old:

> **TAXES:** *The money we must give the government so that it can pay for things like schools, sidewalks, firemen, and policemen.*

Explain to your child that there are different kinds of taxes (personal income, property, corporate, sales). The two that affect your youngster most directly are income tax and sales tax.

Briefly, personal income tax is based on a percentage of one's annual salary and is usually paid to the government on April 15 of every year. Everyone who lives and works in the United States is required to pay taxes.

There are few exceptions; people from other countries who are just visiting the United States for a short time (and not earning income here) do not pay income tax, and people (who are not claimed as dependents by someone else) who do not make a certain amount of money do not have to pay income taxes.

Sales tax is a surcharge that is added onto specific items, like food, clothes, gasoline, and, of course, toys, at the time they are purchased. This will probably be your youngster's first encounter with taxes, and it will come as a most unhappy fact of life if the child first learns about sales tax at the cash register.

If your young son or daughter is saving for a special item, you'll need to explain that they will need not just the price of the toy, but a little more for the sales tax as well.

## HOW TO HELP YOUR CHILD FIGURE OUT SALES TAX

1. First, find out what the sales tax is and note that the sales tax on food purchased in the grocery store may be different from that bought in a restaurant. The figure will be a percentage that is charged per $1. Remember to change the percentage into a workable number by putting a decimal or a .0 in front of it (for example, eight and a half percent is .085).
2. Then multiply that number by the amount of the item.
3. The total, rounded off if necessary, is the correct sales tax.
4. Add the sales tax to the price of the item for the total amount owed.
   EXAMPLE: If your sales tax is 6% and you want to purchase something that costs $13, the total is $13.78 ($13 $\times$ .06 = $.78).

Again, as you practiced with tipping, learning how to figure out the sales tax is a good game to play with a pocket calculator. Give your youngster a fictional total, the percentage that is the sales tax, and let her figure the total on the calculator.

### FAMILY EXERCISE:
### HOW TO SET UP A TAX JAR FOR THE FAMILY

**GOAL:**
To teach children the concept of taxes.
**TOOLS:**
A large jar or container slitted on top for coins.
**RULES:**
Each week upon payment of the allowance, every member of the family must put a percentage of his or her total "income"' into the tax jar. Use what your income tax rate is, so if the child

gets $4 a week for an allowance and your tax bracket is 15 percent, the youngster puts 60 cents into the jar.

At the end of the year, count out how much money has been collected in the tax jar, and as a family, decide how this special money will be spent to benefit the entire group. A trip to the ice cream store? A new board game? Maybe a party? The family tax jar could be a disciplined, fun way for the children to save for something special as well as for the individual child to learn about his or her greater community, the family.

I'm going to briefly discuss other Terrible Ts here and suggest how to explain what they are to your offspring as you do them:

## Tolls

A toll is a charge for using a road. Sometimes there are tolls to cross a bridge or to drive on a highway. The money is usually used to pay for and maintain the road or bridge.

Show your youngster how to watch for upcoming road signs that indicate a toll is coming up. If you can, let him hand the money to the toll booth clerk, or throw the money into an exact-change basket. Explain how exact-change lanes are often faster than the regular lanes.

## Tickets

A ticket is usually a small piece of thick paper or cardboard that shows you have paid for something. (This is not to be confused with the piece of paper a traffic cop gives to a driver!) Here is a list of things that you buy a ticket for:

## THINGS YOU BUY TICKETS FOR

| | | |
|---|---|---|
| Movies | Lunchroom food | Raffles |
| Concerts | Trains/Planes/Buses | Lotteries |
| Plays | Amusement park rides | Ferries |

Most of the time, tickets are used so that the person who helps you, like an usher or a flight attendant, doesn't have to handle money but has proof that you have paid to be there.

The exception is raffles and lotteries, which are completely different types of tickets. Both are really games of chance that you pay to play.

Sometimes it saves you time and/or money to buy several tickets at a time. For instance, at a state fair or an amusement park, you might buy twelve tickets and get a bonus thirteenth. And this saves having to wait in line over and over.

Tickets to certain events like a play or a baseball game will have a specific date on them and can only be used on that date. Movie tickets, however, generally can only be used when they are purchased.

## Tokens

A token is like a ticket in most ways. The main difference is that a token is designed to be accepted by a machine if a person isn't there to take it.

---

## THINGS YOU BUY TOKENS FOR

---

| Bridges | Buses | Streetcars |
| Highways | Subways | Casinos |

---

As with tickets, there are times when it is sensible to purchase tokens in bulk, such as for a bus or subway you take regularly, and times when you may only need one or two tokens, such as for a bridge you only cross occasionally.

Now, those Terrible Ts weren't so terrible after all, were they?

# 8 How to Work with Your Teenager on Money Management

*T*his chapter is devoted exclusively to teenagers. Age-wise, you may have a precocious eleven- or twelve-year-old who is ready for some of the concepts and exercises here. The main focus, however, is on teenagers thirteen to fifteen who are starting to earn (and therefore need to manage) serious money, and on sixteen- to eighteen-year-olds who will soon be off on their own.

I've divided the teenager's list of "must knows" into three areas: budgeting, banking, and advanced concepts (the stock market, mutual funds, and portfolios). But first, here is a money quiz to see exactly how financially savvy your youngster is right now, and what eighteen- or nineteen-year-olds need to be familiar with before they pack their trunk and wave goodbye to start a new phase of independent life.

To start, you, the "professor," need to have your young adult take the following quiz to see which areas you can skip and which you need to focus on more intently:

---

## WHAT TEENAGERS NEED TO KNOW ABOUT MONEY AND MONEY MANAGEMENT BEFORE THEY LEAVE THE NEST

---

1. Do you know how to open a savings account?
   YES _____    NO _____
2. Can you name other kinds of savings vehicles?
   YES _____    NO _____
3. Do you know how to open a checking account?
   YES _____    NO _____
4. Do you know how to balance a checkbook?
   YES _____    NO _____
5. Do you know how to stop payment on a check if necessary?
   YES _____    NO _____
6. Do you know how to reorder checks?
   YES _____    NO _____
7. Can you explain the entries on a bank statement?
   YES _____    NO _____
8. Do you know what your monthly banking fees are for each account?
   YES _____    NO _____
9. Do you know how to buy traveler's checks?
   YES _____    NO _____
10. Can you explain what a wire transfer is?
    YES _____    NO _____
11. Have you earned more than $12 in interest on your savings account this year?
    YES _____    NO _____
12. Can you explain why the interest you pay on a credit card is so important?
    YES _____    NO _____

13. Do you know what the repercussions are if you are late or fail to pay the minimum balance on a credit card?
YES _____      NO _____

14. Could you formulate a livable budget that meets all your expenses without the help of another adult?
YES _____      NO _____

15. Have you stayed on your current budget for at least six months without having to ask a parent for financial help?
YES _____      NO _____

16. Do you know how to read a lease and what to look for before you sign it?
YES _____      NO _____

17. Would you know how to "interview" a prospective roommate (who must be financially responsible)?
YES _____      NO _____

18. Do you know how to get cash quickly in an emergency?
YES _____      NO _____

19. Do you know what to do if you lose your checks or credit card?
YES _____      NO _____

20. Do you know how to take out and renew car insurance?
YES _____      NO _____

21. Do you know how and when to file a state and federal income tax form?
YES _____      NO _____

22. Do you know what a credit union is?
YES _____      NO _____

---

To score, give every yes answer 10 points. If your teen scores below 80, you may need to review previous chapters; if he scores between 90 and 140, he is progressing, but still needs your guidance; and if he scores over 150, you may want to consider hiring him out as a financial consultant!

Totals:   Yes _____   No _____

Score:   _____

Questions 1 to 9 had to do with issues discussed in Chapter 6. Review this chapter with your teenager if this was an area of weakness.

Questions 10 to 16 had to do with budgeting, which was the major focus in Chapter 5. However, I will address formulating a more sophisticated, "guilt-free" budget later in this chapter.

Questions 17 to 22 were concerned with various other financial activities. Some of these I address in this chapter and in Chapters 9 and 10.

## Putting Money Management into Perspective for Your Teenager

Before I get into the specifics of working with your teenager, I want to explain my Time Line Graph. I think it helps to put into perspective how a person might be spending his or her money over a lifetime.

---

### TIME LINE GRAPH

Birth . . . bicycle . . . car . . . college . . . marriage
0 _____ 10 _____ 16 _____ 18 _____ 25 _____

home . . . children . . . children's education . . . own business
28 _____ 30 _____ 35 _____ 38 _____

parents' care . . . retirement
45 _____ 65 _____

---

Let me emphasize that this is just an illustration, not a requirement that everyone *must* be married at twenty-five or start their own business at thirty-eight. Each person's time line will have its own pattern. The purpose of presenting this is to have your teenager think about what her lifetime goals *might* be and plan for them so that she has the financial means to make the dreams come true.

Have a heart-to-heart with your teenager and encourage the youngster to sketch out his or her own Time Line Graph. It's fun to refer to it six months or a year from now, and see if and how the direction has changed.

I urge people to focus on the upcoming goal and to keep an eye on the next few major purchases. For instance, buying a house or a car requires long-term planning.

While buying a home may be the largest single purchase you ever make, it is not the last major financial situation that you will plan and save for. Chances are you still will need to plan for your child's (or children's) education and your retirement at the very least. More than that, you may even have fantasies of someday owning a vacation home somewhere. (And why not?)

## How to Start

You must decide when your teenager is ready to move into "graduate level economics." It may be at the point where the youngster is earning significant money cutting lawns or baby-sitting and needs to manage it more efficiently, or when the precocious offspring has mastered the simple money management exercises we've done earlier in this book and is ready to take on more responsibility.

Certainly by fifteen, your teenager should have reached one of these levels, if not both. Ideally, her savings account is growing regularly and she is staying fairly close to the simple S.O.S. (Savings/Offerings/Spending) budget laid out in Chapter 4.

This qualifies your teenager to move into a more adult-looking budget, and since a budget is the financial road map to get you to where you want to be, I'll be laying out what a typical teenager's budget might look like. Also, I'll show how that budget can be updated into a young adult's budget.

Before we get into the specifics of a teenager's budget, though, you need to consider one major purchase—a college education—that will significantly affect your budget as well as the child's.

## How to Save for a College Education

One of the largest single expenses any of us will undertake is a college education. Think about it. Even at a community college or state university, the average four years of college tuition is going to run at least $20,000, and for an Ivy League school, as high as $100,000—and that's *before* you figure in room and board, books and supplies, clothing, travel, and all the other expenses. Next to a house, a college education is probably the most expensive single item you'll ever pay for.

In some cases, whether a child goes to college or not may depend on what the youngster can contribute financially. Some very bright, achievement-oriented youngsters who have a high grade-point average are confident that some sort of scholarship, grant, or financial aid will help them go to college (there are services that assist in identifying these financial sources). Even if your child is in this elite category, there are still expenses (books, clothes, student fees, socializing) that require money not covered in a scholarship.

As with any major purchase, the sooner you start planning for this possibility, the better. A parent can actually start a college fund when the child is born, but I don't think five or six is too late to start.

If your youngster is already in his early or mid-teens and you have no college fund, then the important question for you and your child is: "Do you need the youngster's financial help to make this purchase happen?"

If the answer is yes, then sit down with the youngster and reevaluate the child's budget in a different light. Where can he increase his outside income? Where can he decrease his spending? Are there large sums of money in savings that would earn more in a CD? Are there scholarships and/or financial aid programs to look into?

The earlier you start planning for college, the better your chances for making it happen.

## How to Set Up a Teenager's Budget

A teenager's budget is going to differ dramatically from a younger child's in two ways: first, you eventually will be turning over all the teen's expenditures to him or her; and second, you will be formulating a precise, detailed budget for your teen.

This does not mean that he must quit school and get a job in order to support himself. It does mean that the funds from your adult budget for clothing, doctor and dentist bills, car insurance, and other living expenses will gradually be turned over to the teenager to dispense (with your supervision). With the exception of shelter (your home), utilities, and whatever meals are eaten at home, your fifteen- to sixteen-year-old should be managing (with your financial help) everything else.

Chances are your youngster has been making all of his or her own *buying* decisions (clothes, books, records, movies) for some time. Now, by turning over your allotment of money to the teenager, you will show her how to make *spending* decisions. After all, wouldn't you prefer to see her start the budgeting process under your roof where you can help?

Take the basic S.O.S. (Savings/Offerings/Spending) budget. Now let's expand all three areas for your teenager, and remember, *you need to look at what is spent or needed over a year's time.*

Savings were divided into short-term and long-term, the latter never to be touched except in an extreme emergency. You and your teen might want to consider starting a two-year-term savings plan for something that the youngster will want or need in two years. Consult the teen's Time Line Graph. Is a car, special camp, or European vacation on his or her time line? The two-year savings plan will be designated for this goal.

Now, on offerings, does the teenager want to redirect the charitable givings to a different organization? That's allowed! An adult-looking budget should have adult-looking charities. Perhaps an organization that helps runaway teens or an AIDS support group would be more meaningful now.

What should be added to offerings is a section for gifts. Chances are, your teenager is carrying a heavier responsibility in this area than a child would. Figure out how much more a week he or she needs to be contributing here.

Finally, spending. Clearly, this is the area that will change the most. Start by making a list of all "money in" and "money out" entries. Money in includes the child's allowance, odd jobs, summer and after-school jobs, and gifts of money. The money out list covers meal money, all aspects of transportation (gas for car, car insurance, if applicable), school and drugstore (shampoo, deodorant, toothpaste, pantyhose, etc.) supplies, entertainment, and clothing. *Do not differentiate between what you currently pay for and what the teenager pays for.*

(You need to think about all the areas where you spend money on the child. Include things like dentist and doctor visits, and one-time expenses like cheerleading or sports uniforms. Put these items on the list.)

Now, together with your youngster, assign a dollar figure to each entry on both lists. A typical fifteen-year-old's list might look something like this:

## SAMPLE MONEY IN/MONEY OUT LIST

**Money In**

Weekly Allowance
(at $15/week) $780/year

Odd Jobs
($10/week) $520/year

After-School Job
(for 36 weeks at $25/week)
$900/year

Summer Job
(for 14 weeks at $75/week)
$1,050/year

Gifts of Money
$100

**Money Out**

Food Allowance
(for 36 weeks at $20/week
during school year only)
$720/year

Transportation
(bicycle repairs) $100/year

School/Drugstore Supplies
$1,040/year

Clothing
$1,200/year

Entertainment
$1,000/year

Dentist/Doctor
$320/year

College Fund
$350/year

Savings
$750/year

Offerings
$300/year

Total: $3,350                    Total: $5,780

Now, with your teenager, cross off the expenses (money out) that you are not ready to turn over to the child or that it's not practical to turn over (like doctors' bills that get paid directly by your insurance company).

With that new total, you and your child can determine what the difference is between the two figures ($2,430) and how to bridge that gap. Does the parent need to increase the allowance? Does the child need to cut back on the expenses? Probably both.

This example of money in/money should include whatever additional financial responsibilities you and your teenager may have agreed upon in the savings and offerings categories, but double-check those figures. In theory, those increases should be covered in the allowance, so be prepared, Mom and Dad—this is the figure that will undoubtedly go up significantly.

Finally, now that you have a year-long overview of the teen's total budget, you need to work out how this money gets paid to the youngster. Is it in weekly, monthly, or quarterly installments? For things like drugstore supplies, weekly may be preferable.

However, think about giving the kid his clothing allowance in larger sums twice a year, once before the school year starts and again in the spring. The clothing allowance is a good budget to break out separately. You should work with your youngster to help him decide what to buy and when.

This budget will instantly stop the I-need-designer-jeans-or-I'll-die-syndrome. Your teenager can buy the jeans, and then deal with the consequences if she doesn't have enough money left over for other things. The process may be painful to watch, but stick to your guns! The lessons of choice and responsibility are invaluable.

## Teenagers and Banking

At this point, your teenager should be familiar with basic banking services and should already have his or her own savings account. By age fifteen or sixteen, the youngster is ready for a checking account (see Chapter 5). So, the next adult financial items your teenager needs to learn about are credit cards and the stock market.

The word "credit" comes from the Latin word "creditus," meaning "entrusted." When someone lends you money, he or she is trusting you to repay it. Credit is not a right, it is a privilege. You have to earn the right to have credit and you must show you are responsible in order to get credit or a credit card.

Credit means that someone will lend you money and give you time to pay it back, usually for an added fee. Credit enables you to buy now and pay later. When a bank lends you money, it is giving you credit. Consumers use credit to buy the things they need, like houses, clothes, cars, and for emergencies. Businesses use credit to expand and grow. Even governments use credit to build roads or bridges or to run the town, city, state, or country.

Sometimes you are the one that gives credit. For example, when you buy a U.S. savings bond, you are lending the government money. The government promises to pay you back the amount you lent them, plus interest, at a later date.

Various sources—banks, businesses, stores, and individuals—can give credit. A store that gives credit allows you to buy now and pay later. A repairperson who mends something and then sends you a bill is giving you credit. He or she trusts you to pay the bill. A local grocery store, for example, may give a good customer credit by letting that person buy things and pay later.

Banks give credit through installment loans, lines of credit, overdraft lines of credit, mortgages, and credit cards. Before a bank will give credit, it will run a credit check to make sure that the person pays his or her debts. A bank will only give credit to someone it feels sure will pay back the loan.

Department stores offer a form of credit called *installment credit*. For instance, if you buy a sofa for $700 on credit from the store, you repay the $700, plus interest, over a period of time. Each payment is called an *installment*. This allows you to charge what you need now and pay it back regularly over time.

The major down side to a credit card is the interest you must pay. Unless you pay the full amount owed on your credit card each month, you must pay interest, thus making the goods or services you buy with a credit card more expensive than those you pay for with cash. This is because the interest you pay each month is added to the cost of your purchases.

Many stores and companies issue credit cards that can only be used at their establishments. Only banks and other financial institutions can issue cards that can be used at any place that accepts those particular bank credit cards.

A department store credit card, though, is a good card for a teenager to begin with. Unless your teen has his or her own sitcom on TV, however, you will probably need to open the account for the child.

You and your teenager should discuss which store is appropriate and then pick up an application for a credit card there. If you already have a credit card with the store, talk to someone in the credit department about obtaining a second card in the child's name. You also may want to have a charge limit on it that is even lower than what the store will allow, at least to start.

Another possibility instead of a credit card is something called a "secured card." This is where you pay a deposit of money, say $500, and then the cardholder can charge up to that limit. After a cardholder has shown that he or she is responsible, then they can be issued a credit card.

Each month when the bill comes in, review it with your teenager. Make sure she purchased everything that is charged on the card, and then decide if she should make a full or partial payment on the bill.

A bank card like Visa or MasterCard is harder to get, but it is a valuable one for a teenager who is traveling or going away to college to have in case of an emergency.

If your teenager has a longtime savings account with a bank, is gainfully employed at least part-time, and you, the parent, do your banking there also, it is reasonable to expect the bank will consider giving the teenager a credit card of some kind. It may be in your name or co-signed by you. Meet with the credit officer at your bank and see what kind of card is practicable for your teenager.

A credit card that is used responsibly by a young adult can help him or her build a positive credit history. If abused, it can destroy a person's credit record. Emphasize that a bad credit record is very hard to fix and takes years to do. Unlike that F you got in gym class years ago, a bad credit report will not be forgotten and, in fact, will follow you wherever you go.

## Your Teenager and the Stock Market

After your child has mastered banking and using credit cards responsibly, he or she might be ready to step into the world of investing and the stock market.

The stock market was created, in part, so that the general public could invest their money, and perhaps make money, in a company they believed held promise. On the other side of the coin, the stock market system can help a company that is publicly traded (offers stock to the public) gain additional financial support, which is sometimes used to improve and expand the business.

There is a little Donald Trump in all of us and buying

stock, or a little piece of a company, is a good alternative for people who can't afford to buy a whole company.

Here is a teenager's definition of stock:

> **STOCK:** *A small piece of a company that can be purchased. The piece of paper that shows ownership of stock is called a* stock certificate, *and it is issued only by the company. Stock certificates are bought and sold at the* stock market. *The people who buy and sell stock are called* stockbrokers, *and the people who own stock are called* stockholders.

As with saving and spending money, the same principle of discipline applies to investing in the stock market: use common sense. Consider allowing your child to take a portion of his savings (say 20 percent) to invest in the market.

There are two ways he or she can do this: either design a portfolio or invest in a mutual fund. I'll go into more detail on both in the next sections.

## How to Design Your Own Portfolio

The fun of following the stock market is a little like watching what your favorite sports team or movie star is doing. You become interested in the company/team/star and track their successes and failures.

A good way to start to learn about a company is to have your teenager pick one that he or she identifies with in some way. Here are some questions to help a teen determine this:

---

### SAMPLE QUESTIONS TO HELP DETERMINE INTEREST IN A COMPANY

---

1. What company makes your favorite brand of sneakers?
2. What toys or video games are hot and what is the name of the company that makes them?

---

3. What company makes your favorite cold cereal?
4. What is the name of the movie studio that produced the last movie you enjoyed?
5. What is the name of the company that produced your favorite CD?
6. What is your favorite store to shop in?
7. What is your favorite restaurant?
8. Who makes your favorite car?

Some of these answers will lead you and your teen to the name of some parent companies, such as Mattel or General Motors, that are publicly traded on the stock market. (You can see which companies are publicly traded by checking the daily newspaper's business section where the stock market is listed.) With this final list of companies, you and your teen have just built a consumer-driven portfolio of stocks.

The next step is to pick a stock and purchase a few shares in the company through a stockbroker. (You may buy just a single share of stock, but this is generally frowned upon.) If your youngster is under twenty-one, you will need to buy the stock and then give it to your teenager, or you can buy them jointly in both your names (the teen will need a Social Security number for tax purposes).

When you buy shares of individual stock, you and your child will receive, as stockholders, a copy of the company's *annual report*. This is a formal report, much like a term paper, that publicly owned companies must issue each year to explain how the company is doing, what its new products or services are, and what its financial or expansion goals are for the following year.

When you get this (it will take a few weeks to be mailed to you) go through the annual report with your teenager. Most reports are written so that a lay audience can understand them, and it should make you feel like one of the owners!

Even though your child cannot actually buy and sell stock, you can involve him in the process. Teach your child to find his or her stocks listed in the business section of the newspaper. Each stock is listed by its name. However, most of the names are abbreviated. For example, Disney is "Disney," but McDonald's is "McDonld" and Toys R Us is "ToyRU."

The numbers and abbreviations can be confusing at first, but eventually your eye will get used to them and be able to find things quickly. Here is a sample listing from *The Wall Street Journal*. Though each paper prints the information a little differently, most of the information is the same. (One note: while expressed in fractions and decimals, the numbers below really represent dollars and cents. For instance, 52⅝ is $52.625 and 41¼ is $41.25.)

---

## NEW YORK STOCK EXCHANGE
## COMPOSITE TRANSACTION
### (as seen in *The Wall Street Journal*)

---

| 52 weeks | | | | | Yld | | Vol | | | | Net |
|---|---|---|---|---|---|---|---|---|---|---|---|
| Hi | Lo | Stock | Sym | Div | % | PE | 100s | Hi | Lo | Close | Chg |
| 52⅝ | 41¼ | ParCom | PCI | .80 | 1.6 | 24 | 4205 | 51⅜ | 50 | 51¼ | +1⅛ |

**52 weeks Hi/Lo:** the highest and lowest price of the stock over the last 52 weeks.

**Stock:** ParCom is the abbreviation for the company, Paramount Communications.

**Sym:** PCI is the ticker symbol for the stock.

**Div:** Cash dividend per share, given in dollars and cents. A dividend is a payment to the stockholder of part of the company's profits. A PCI stockholder would receive $.80 for each share owned.

---

**Yld %:** Percent yield is a way of expressing the stock's current value; it tells you how much dividend you get for what you pay. For the percent yield of PCI, you divide $.80 by $51.25 to get 1.6%

**PE:** The abbreviation for price/earnings ratio. It refers to the relationship between the price of one share of stock and the yearly earnings of the company. Earnings are not given in the stock listings, so you can't calculate the PE ratio from the chart.

**Vol 100s:** Shows the volume of shares traded the day before the listing appears. To get that number you multiply the listed number times 100. Yesterday, 4,205,000 shares of PCI were traded.

**Hi, Lo** and **Close:** These listings tell you the stock's highest, lowest, and closing prices for the previous day. The highest price paid for PCI was 51⅜, the lowest was 50, and the price at the close of the market was 51¼.

**Net Chg:** Net change compares the closing price given here with the closing price of the day before. PCI went up 1⅛ point.

## How the Stock Market Works

The stock market works on the principle of supply and demand. For instance, if there are not a lot of Mickey Mantle baseball cards (the supply is low), and lots of people want one (the demand is high), then the price goes up. On the other hand, if a store has a lot of brown bananas (high supply) and no one wants rotten bananas (low demand) the price goes way down.

The market works the same way. If lots of people want a stock because the company is earning money, the price goes up. If a company is not coming out with popular, hot products and its earnings are down, people don't want to buy that stock, and so the price goes down.

## How to Buy Stock

In theory, investors can go directly to a company to buy stock. The law does not require that you go through a stockbroker. However, it is impractical to do it yourself.

A stockbroker is a person licensed to buy and sell stock for other people. Some brokers just buy and sell the stock you ask them to buy or sell. They are called *discount brokers*. They charge a small fee. Other brokers give advice and answer your questions about stock and help you find the stock that will suit your needs. They charge a little more.

In order to buy and sell stock, you have to open an account with your broker. It is much like opening a bank account. Once the account is opened, most brokers will let you buy and sell stock over the telephone. Each month you will receive a statement from your broker that is similar to a bank statement. It will tell you what you have bought and sold, what the stock is worth, and what the total fees are.

## The Stock Market

In the olden days, people used to stand at the street corner to buy and sell stock. In fact, in the late eighteenth century, a group of stock traders would get together in New York City under a tree to work. In 1792, they founded the New York Stock Exchange near that site as a place where buyers and sellers could come together.

Today, most stock trading of the largest corporations in the United States is done on the New York Stock Exchange (NYSE, or "Big Board," as it is also called). The stock of more than 1,800 companies is traded on the NYSE and trading volume is usually over 100 million shares per day.

The traders meet face-to-face on the floor of the exchange and conduct an auction of buying and selling based on supply and demand.

## How to Explain Mutual Funds to Your Teen

If you don't want to buy and sell your own stock, investment companies can pool your money with other people's money to form a *mutual fund*. The mutual fund is then invested in different stocks or bonds. (A bond is a certificate you receive when you lend the government or a company money.)

Each mutual fund has a goal; some want only to invest in the best and largest companies, called *blue chip stocks*. (Blue chip stock, by the way, got its name from the blue poker chips that are worth the most money.) Other mutual funds may have a goal to invest only in a certain type of stock, like utilities, or drug companies, or entertainment companies.

The value of the fund changes according to how the stocks in the fund are performing. The person who runs the fund may buy and sell stock.

Mutual fund ownership comes in the form of shares, so as a shareholder in a fund, you receive the gains or losses as long as you own shares.

There are many reasons why people like to invest in mutual funds. One is that as an individual investor, you might not have as much time to follow the stock market as the person who runs the fund. Another advantage of a mutual fund is that as a part of a larger group, you have the potential of earning a larger profit. Most people can't afford to invest in each of the many companies that a mutual fund might offer.

You can invest in a mutual fund with a small amount of money, sometimes as low as $100 to $500.

You purchase participation in a mutual fund through your broker, just like stock. You may buy it jointly with your teenager or buy it and give it to her. Each month, you will receive a statement from your mutual fund. It will show the performance and how much you are earning.

Work with your teenager and have him keep a list of the stocks and/or mutual funds that are owned. Each quarter, ask the youngster to report to you how the portfolio is doing.

### Explaining Life's Little Bummers to Your Teen

When I speak to large groups about financial planning, there are generally two areas the audience cites as their major budget-busters. These are taxes and insurance.

All of us over the age of twenty-one know that we are going to have to pay taxes and probably several different kinds of insurance. Intellectually, we know this, but emotionally, these are tough expenses to shell out money for because most of us feel we get little in return.

Like it or not, taxes and insurance are realities and they need to be covered in a budget.

# 9 What Parents Need to Tell a Child About Their Own Finances

*I*n my mother's day, and my grandmother's before that, a family discussion on the subject of sex or money was not considered "appropriate dinner conversation." Both were viewed by them to be intimate, private topics, and there is evidence to suggest that neither subject was discussed much even between husbands and wives!

As we head into a new century, social mores have been relaxed and sex is even a required topic of discussion within families. The great life-threatening dangers that can come from imprudent or unprotected sex have forced most parents out of Victorian Age restraints.

The subject of money has not been equally discussed, yet the dangers of imprudent or unprotected spending have their own serious consequences: personal bankruptcy and, at the extreme, homelessness are some of the unfortunate results that are on the rise.

By this chapter, you hopefully have reached a higher comfort level on the subject of money than your own parents may have had with you. And, ideally, you are actively working and talking to your children about money.

However, are you prepared to discuss your own finances with your child? "Too personal" or "None of the child's business!" you say? Perhaps. No parent cares to pass along information about him or herself that can be used to embarrass them by the child later on. (That's why we discourage Grandma from displaying our old report cards!)

I do not believe that your child needs to know that you once bounced seven checks in one day, or that you were denied a mortgage four times before finally getting one. However, there is some financial information about yourself that an older child, and certainly a teenager, does need to be aware of for their own benefit.

Almost all of this need-to-know information centers around the financial planning for the future that you and your spouse have done, particularly in the event of your untimely death. Whether you reveal to your youngster what your annual income is or how much you spend on rent or mortgage is your personal choice. The area the youngster does need to be aware of is how you've planned to provide for the child if something happens to you and/or your spouse.

What follows here is a discussion of your personal financial activities, and some suggestions on how and when to explain them to your children without scaring or overwhelming them.

### *Your Will and Its Importance to Your Child*

Your will may be the single most important document you ever create for your child. Not only does a will outline what happens to your financial assets and designate an executor (the person who sees that the instructions in a will are carried out), it also lays out (or should) what you want to happen with your children until they are old enough to be on their own.

It is shocking to me to learn that despite the obvious importance of having a will, two out of three Americans die without one. The lack of a proper will, however, puts your loved ones and assets in serious jeopardy if something happens to you.

Many parents, however, do draw up, or revise, their wills when a child is born. If you did it with your first, remember to revise it with each additional child. And if you haven't done it, DO IT TODAY! Very bad things happen to kids if they suddenly lose their parents and there is no will dictating who cares for them and how.

A lawyer can draw up a basic will for under $100. There are books available that show you how to write your own will and have it notarized so that it is a legitimate legal document. At the very least, you can write a will out by hand outlining who you want to get custody of your child, who gets what assets, and so forth. (You should sign and date it, put it in a safe place, and give copies to a trusted family member outside your household such as a friend or clergyperson.)

Some handwritten wills can stand up in court, even if they are contested. The safest will, of course, is the one done by a lawyer who specializes in this area and knows the laws of your state.

Keep in mind that in the vast majority of families, the surviving relatives or guardians *want* to abide by the parents' wishes if they know what those desires are. So, if you don't have a will at the moment, sketch something out on paper immediately, or discuss it with a close friend so that your instructions are known to someone until you get a formal will.

---

## THINGS GOVERNING YOUR CHILD
## THAT YOU NEED TO ADDRESS IN YOUR WILL

---

1. Who will be the executor of the will? This needs to be someone you trust to make sure that all your affairs are handled according to your specific instructions.
2. Who should get custody or guardianship of your child or children in the event of one or both parents' death? Discuss this decision carefully with your spouse and maybe the older children, then with the prospective guardian (there may be a reason you don't know about that would prevent the designated person from taking on this responsibility). Generally, if there is no will and the courts must decide who gets your children, they will go to a blood relative (and Great Aunt Sarah may not be who you want to raise your kids!).
3. How will the child be provided for financially? Check to see if your assets and insurance policies are sufficient to provide for the rearing and education of your children.
4. How are your assets to be divided up? Who is to get what? Do you want the child to receive all of the money when he or she reaches maturity, or do you want to space the payments out? (A lawyer can explain your options.)

---

After you have written a basic will, you and your lawyer should review it every five years or so. Things change. You buy a house, have more babies, have more assets that need to be divided, and these things need updating in the will.

## *What You Should Tell Your Child About Your Will*

The reason a discussion with your child about your will is so valuable is that it gives you the chance to assure the youngster that he or she will be taken care of if something should happen to you and your spouse—and don't think your four- or five-year-old hasn't wondered about this.

From the time they are quite young, your children hear terrible stories about what happens to boys and girls without parents. Where, after all, were Cinderella's parents? Or Goldilocks's? And think about the awful things that happened to Hansel and Gretel or Charles Dickens's Oliver.

Your young ones need to be assured that even if you aren't there to care for them, you have provided for them to be loved and cared for by someone else.

The overriding thought you want to convey is that you have planned for the child to be cared for, emotionally and financially, by someone, and that this plan is laid out in something called a will.

The subject of your mortality is not a pleasant one to you or your child, and while I encourage forthright discussions in most areas, this is one you will want to move gently on, especially with younger kids.

The subject came up in my family in a very odd way. My sister Alison lives nearby on a farm, and when my daughter, Kyle, was about four, a mare of Alison's died after giving birth. We were frantically calling around the county to find another nursing mare when my teary-eyed daughter asked me what would become of her and Rhett if something happened to me.

While the question did surprise me, it proved to be an appropriate time to assure the child that she and her brother would be taken care of, and, in fact, there was a detailed plan (the will) that was already in place. When we got home, Kyle insisted on seeing the will and even though she could not read all of it, it did seem to reassure her that she would not end up in an orphanage begging for porridge if I died.

I feel confident in saying that the right opportunity to discuss the existence of your will will present itself. Children are curious about death and always have a lot of questions for you about it from the time they are four or five.

You will see an opening in one of these conversations to

add that everybody dies sometime, and while you plan to live for a very, very long time, if something ever happened to you, the youngster would *not* be put out on the street to live.

Children under the age of seven are probably too young to go into any detail about the will. Undoubtedly, they will want to know some specifics like who will take care of them and where they will live. Again, it should be reassuring to the child to know that there is a well-thought-out plan for his or her future.

Here is a young child's definition of a will. (Please note that this is not an adult's definition, which is more concerned with the distribution of your estate, but a child's definition as it relates to him or her.)

**WILL:** *A written plan that lays out how a child will be cared for if something happens to the parents.*

Your child already knows that you carefully plan ahead of time who will take care of him after school if you're not there, on Saturday nights if you go out, and if you and your spouse go out of town together on business or a vacation. Explain that a will is just an extension of that same kind of planning.

I would emphasize to a young one that, in all probability, this plan will not be used until you are a very old person and the child is grown up. It is there, however, to protect the child just in case of an emergency.

With grade-school children, you may want to go into a bit more detail about the will and where it is located. Teenage children should be made more familiar with the will and specifically what their responsibilities are if there are younger children.

## How to Explain Insurance to Children

Life insurance, which is just one of many kinds of insurance, relates to a will in that both are designed to care for surviving children in one way or another.

I will not get into a lengthy discussion of insurance here. Instead, I will offer a child's definition of insurance for you to use and some areas of insurance that you might want to discuss with your youngster as you talk about wills.

Here is a definition of insurance for young ones:

> **INSURANCE:** *An agreement where an insurance company pays you money if something bad happens.*

For youngsters age nine to eighteen:

> **INSURANCE:** *A contract purchased in advance to guarantee compensation for a specific loss by fire, theft, death, or other mishap.*

There are many different kinds of insurance, from contact lens and car insurance to disability and life insurance. With most insurance policies, you take out the insurance and then pay a *premium* once a year for as long as you want the policy.

*Life insurance* is usually a large sum of money (several thousands of dollars) that is paid to the *beneficiary* upon the death of the person insured. If you and your spouse both carry life insurance (and you should if you have children), explain to the youngster that this money will go to help support them if something happens to either parent.

For older children and teenagers, it would be helpful to show them where the insurance policies are kept, and the name of the insurance agent, in case they need to help take care of these details in your absence.

## *Your Personal, Household, and Family Finances*

There may be a wide spectrum of financial activities you are handling that, because you handle them exclusively, only you know about. This can include everything from the day-to-day household expenses and bills to safe-deposit boxes and financial portfolios.

Undoubtedly you have heard the horror stories of older women who suddenly lost their husbands and had absolutely no idea what their financial stituation was, or even where to look to find out. It is a cruel and totally unnecessary situation.

You should be communicating with your spouse your activities if you are the principal bookkeeper and financial planner in the family. The nonparticipating spouse should take the responsibility of knowing where the financial records are kept.

If you are a single parent, you need to keep careful records so that if your executor or the child's guardian comes in to settle your affairs, that person can determine the status of bills, financial portfolios, and such. The adult will need to know where these records are kept, and I would say that if your youngster is over the age of seven or eight, she can direct the person to the correct drawer or file cabinet with the records. If the children are younger, tell another family member, or the designated guardian, where the records are kept.

I also recommend that your teenage children be told generally what these financial arrangements are, and definitely where important documents and records are kept.

Here is a list of household financial documents that your family needs to be able to find in your absence:

---

### IMPORTANT FINANCIAL DOCUMENTS
### IN YOUR HOME

---

Bills
Bank statements
Canceled checks

---

Deed to house
Titles and registrations to all vehicles
Tax returns
Insurance policies
Health insurance cards
Wills
Financial portfolio
Pension plan information

*(Nondocuments)*
Combination of home safe
Important keys, including safe-deposit box key
Location of bank accounts
Credit union accounts
Location of fur vault
Personal address book

---

Some people keep many of these documents either in strong boxes or in home safes, or they keep them at the office. Let someone know if these important items are somewhere other than your desk drawers at home.

## Trust Funds for Your Child

A trust fund is money that is kept for the benefit of another person, usually a child. I will not go into detail about how to set up a trust fund in this book—your banker or lawyer can help you with that. I mention it here, though, for two reasons: first, as a suggestion to parents who are drawing up financial plans for their children, and second, as a reminder to review your intentions for the trust fund with your youngster.

Many people believe that trust funds are something only for very, very wealthy children. This isn't true today. For instance, parents can create a trust fund specifically for college that becomes available to a child when he or she turns eighteen. Then, if something happens to the parents before the child reaches the designated age, the executor of the will sees that the trust fund is carried out.

Again, the existence of a trust is something you should mention to your grade-schooler and describe in greater detail to your teenager.

## Your Hidden Assets

Take a few minutes and carefully think about other, hidden assets you may have. Do you keep a significant amount of cash secreted away somewhere in the house? Is there expensive jewelry, stock certificates, or bonds at home? Is there a large personal loan that a close friend or family member is repaying you?

These are all additional assets that are part of your estate and would belong to your heirs as you have directed in your will. They do not have to be in your formal will; just keep a written record somewhere among your important papers.

## How to Explain Other Family Crises

In addition to death, there are other substantial crises that can affect a family emotionally and financially. Again, it is better to have these conversations with your youngster *before* the crisis.

### DIVORCE.

Unless you're Amish, your school-age child has probably heard the word "divorce." Child psychiatrists say that this is a trauma that can last a youngster all his or her life if not handled properly.

Very often, a large part of the trauma is connected with

money (a leading cause of divorce according to the statistics). With a divorce, the custodial parent, usually the mother, sometimes can no longer afford to live where the family was, so they must move to a new environment. On top of that, the large majority of mothers must go back to work, and child-care arrangements often change drastically.

These may or may not be the realities that play out for you. My strong advice here is to explain to the child in advance what divorce is, and how it might affect him, and then reassure the youngster that you will take care of him as best you can.

### REMARRIAGE.

Experts say most young children want to know how this event is going to affect them in very simple terms. Which bedroom will they sleep in? What will their name be?

More often than not, the new marriage will represent an easing of the financial burden the single parent was carrying. The positive financial aspects of this change can help to lessen the trauma, so try to point out those positives to the youngster.

### JOB LOSS AND LAYOFF.

This is certainly an emergency situation and one where young-sters have the potential of being helpful. Whether the job loss or layoff was anticipated or a surprise, explain to the child that the whole family will have to work together until this crisis is over.

Discuss how this setback will affect the family in general, and the child in particular. Will he or she have to give up ballet lessons? Does the job loss mean the family will become homeless? Youngsters usually have real fears that need to be addressed promptly.

Talk to your children about what they can do to help in this situation. Kids want to help because it makes them feel more in control and needed. Perhaps the child would like to suspend his or her allowance or donate it toward the family's support? Or, is there a chore or job that the child can help with or take over, such as baby-sitting or gardening?

Kids can be creative. When the husband of one of my best friends lost his job a month before Christmas, her children donated all their gift money to the family account, and gave "gift chits" instead of presents. One chit was for breakfast in bed for five Sundays, another was for ten hours of silence (which the parent would designate), and one was for twenty hours of free baby-sitting services. My friend liked the presents so much, she's asking for the same gifts this year!

**JOB RELOCATION.**

Usually a job relocation is due to a promotion for a parent, and therefore a raise. These are positive points to make to a young one upset about leaving his best friend or favorite teacher. Explain that it is a trade-off where the family gives up one thing to move to something better.

## What You Need to Know about Your Parents' Finances

Now that you've updated your spouse and offspring about your financial situation, what do you know about your own parents' financial affairs?

Sociologists call people who have both children and parents still alive the "sandwich generation." This term was coined for the growing group of middle-aged parents who must care for both children and ailing parents at the same time.

If your parents are alive, whether ailing or healthy, you should be familiar with what their wishes and plans are for the future. You may have responsibilities to carry out, and/or there could be significant financial repercussions that would directly affect your family.

Generally, without going into great detail, the main questions you need to ask your parents are: "What are your wishes upon your death?" and "How would you want to see the surviving spouse cared for?"

You should know the same information about your parents' will, insurance, and estate as your teenager knows about your own. Ask your parents where their will and other important documents (deeds, tax reports, auto registrations, etc.) are kept.

Another important "What if . . . ?" question you need to discuss with your parents is what happens if they become disabled or can no longer live on their own. Do they want to go into a nursing home? Do they want to live with you or another relative? Perhaps they would want their house sold, and a separate wing for them built onto your house, for example.

Many people, particularly older parents, have very specific ideas on how they want their funeral handled and where they want to be buried. Discuss these wishes with your parent or parents, and get the information you need.

Given the range of possibilities in the issues raised here—many affecting your finances and lifestyle—it is better to discuss them with your parents *before* the need arises.

# 10 How to Negotiate Living with Your Adult Children

*Hot news flash:* The number of parents suffering from Empty Nest Syndrome has been greatly reduced in the 1990s.

That's the good news. The not-so-good news to lots of parents is that the reason many procreators are not struggling with Empty Nest Syndrome is they never get that opportunity. Recent Census Bureau figures show two remarkable facts: more adult children are staying in the parental home longer before moving out on their own, and many adult children are *returning* to the ancestral home after living away.

The reason for both of these trends is almost entirely economic; the adult child simply cannot afford to live independently.

The tragedy is that many of these adult children are not in their late teens or early twenties. I know of a former colleague who recently moved his family of six in with his elderly parents because he had lost his job, and after a year still had not found employment. It was traumatic for everyone involved.

If your grown offspring (temporarily) fails at the American Dream and must choose between a welfare hotel or your home, what can you do?

There is hardly anyone I know who could say no to a child who needed to move back home, but there are ways the two generations can help to make the cohabitation bearable.

First, formulate a *lease* between yourself and your offspring. It does not have to be drawn up by a lawyer; all you need is a written agreement that the two of you reach on how you will live together.

## Why Draw Up a Lease Between Parent and Adult Children?

The point of the lease is to lay out rules that you both agree upon so that you lessen the friction or unpleasantness later on. (It is similar to a prenuptial contract in some ways.)

For the offspring who chooses to stay in your household after high school or college, this agreement helps to establish him as an adult in your eyes. It says to him that you recognize him as an adult with certain freedoms and responsibilities. (You might have to lift the 11 P.M. curfew on the child, but you also get to relinquish doing his or her laundry.)

For the adult child moving back in, a lease discourages any illusion that you are a hotel and the lodging comes with free maid service. Your child may actually welcome an agreement that lays out what his obligations are because it reduces feelings of dependence and helplessness. Even if a youngster cannot share the full financial burden of running a household, she can help with the physical chores.

Here are some guidelines on what should be addressed in this lease. With a few exceptions, most of the points in this agreement have no right or wrong answer. Things like a time limit on how long the child stays under a parent's roof and who pays for what differ greatly from family to family.

## How to Set Up a Lease with Your Adult Child

This lease should be formed at the point when the teenager or young adult has entered the work force and decided to wait before leaving home, or prior to when the adult child moves back into your house. It is much harder to break old habits after the child has established residency.

Remember that in this case you are the landlord and the child is the tenant. While you want to relate to your offspring as an adult, you do have certain prerogatives that the child does not.

Here is a short list of questions that you, the landlord, need to ask yourself and your spouse to first establish what you feel is fair to request of your child. These questions focus on the trouble areas that normally come up in a household. Many of these points actually would be addressed in an apartment lease, so it is not unreasonable for you, the landlord, to focus on them.

---

### WORKSHEET FOR PARENTS ABOUT TO BECOME LANDLORDS

---

1. Should the child pay rent?
   Yes _____ No _____
2. How much rent should the child pay?
   $ _____ if employed; $ _____ if unemployed
3. Should the child pay a rental deposit?
   Yes _____ and it should be _____ months' rent
   No _____

4. Should this lease be for a specific time period?
   Yes _____ for _____ year(s), to be renewed, if necessary
   No _____

5. How do you divide utilities?
   Electricity __-__ (percentage, e.g., 50-50, 60-40)
   Water __-__ (percentage)
   Telephone __-__ (percentage of monthly service charge)
   plus all of the child's long distance charges
   Other _____

6. What household chores is the child responsible for?
   Indoors _____ (garbage disposal, dusting, vacuuming, etc.)
   Outdoors _____ (raking leaves, shoveling snow, painting house, etc.)

7. Is your child allowed to use your car?
   Yes _____        No _____
   If yes, who pays for gas and insurance?

8. Where does child park his/her car?
   Garage/Driveway/Street/Other _____

9. Is your child allowed to have pets (or additional pets)?
   Yes _____        No _____

10. Are overnight guests allowed?
    Yes _____        No _____

11. May your child eat your groceries?
    Yes _____ and he/she contributes $__ to budget
    No _____

12. Who prepares the meals?

---

This is not a quiz, so there are no right or wrong answers. It is a list that should get you started on deciding what goes into your lease or agreement with your children.

Every family has additional subjects that need to be addressed, such as smokers versus nonsmokers, when and where guests may be entertained, how telephone messages are taken and distributed. Think about these and other issues that might need to be addressed here.

The next step is to write out the lease with the decisions you and your spouse have made and believe fair, and then discuss it with your child/tenant. As always, be willing to negotiate. Perhaps your offspring would be willing to take on the responsibility of seeing that your car was properly maintained for the privilege of parking her car in the garage.

This lease also might serve as a good format to share with a young adult in an apartment with a roommate. They will have similar questions they need to work out before moving in together.

## How to Enforce the Lease

I would hope that you never have to go beyond a simple reminder to the child/tenant when there are infractions of your agreement. The strain of open warfare is too much for most of us.

If there are problems with compliance, go back and think about what a landlord does in these cases. Usually there are three steps that can be taken: a written warning, a financial penalty, and then eviction.

I know of one instance where the parents were finally forced to insist that their son, his wife, and four children move out of the house because of the severe strain it was putting on the older couple's health. I also know of a couple who eventually decided to give their house to their three live-in adult sons and move into a nearby condo.

More often, however, I hear of parents who will give their grown offspring a brief safe haven from the harsh world while the adult child redirects his or her life after a divorce or job change. It usually works out well. (Of course, it helps if the parent has a *very* big house!)

# Epilogue:
## One Final Word—
## "Go Forth and Multiply"

---

*I*n many ways, I feel I've just scratched the surface on the subject of teaching your child about money. Finance is not an uncomplicated field of study; no single book could cover all there is to know. Money management is a subject that you and your child should continue to explore for as long as you both use it—which might be until the day you die at the ripe old age of 108! I hope this book has shown you how and when to begin.

Be patient with your little ones (and even more so with your teenagers). Most of all, make every effort to keep the learning process light and *fun!* Dealing with money is a challenge most of us face throughout our lifetime, and you, the parent, can greatly influence how your child approaches finance. Will it be with confidence or fear? The

---

answer depends largely on you, both as the teacher and the role model.

Does that mean your child's "financial literacy," as I call it, hinges on you? Yes, it does. Much depends on your persistence in explaining the thousand little nuances—from why you leave a tip for the waitress to how the fluctuation in interest rates affects you—to your youngster day after day after day. Don't make money management a passing fad in your household; make it a lifestyle.

As you work with your youngster, whatever his or her age, ask yourself this question often: "What do I tell my child about finance that I wish someone had told me at that age?" My experience has been that some of the best teachers of financial management have been those who have suffered the most at the hands of money mismanagement. Use your past mistakes with money (and who doesn't have a wealth of those to draw on?) to alert your children to the many pitfalls they will face and can avoid.

With the exception of health issues, I personally believe that there are few worries worse than those dealing with money. Many of us will have a brush with impending financial disaster once or twice during our lifetime. Things like unexpected hospital bills, once-a-century hurricanes, and/or a surprise property tax bill can twist a sensible, working budget into a pretzel. However, the strong foundation that you lay with the basics in this book can go miles in sparing your child from frequent bouts with the money blues.

Here's an easy way to check your progress with your child: from time to time, after the basics are laid out, run down the list of words in the Glossary and see how many the youngster knows. This should indicate the areas of finance that need further explanation.

In the end, all of us have to learn to "just say no" when the urge to spend money hits. Until a solid nest egg is built (that will go far in protecting one from life's constant emergencies), veto all unnecessary trips to the mall, cancel all nights out on the town, even forgo that single package of gum until the financial goal is reached. With a comfortable nest egg, solid management skills, and a pound of self-control, almost anyone will be able to deal with most financial surprises that arise. It's not so hard. You can do this for yourself and your child.

Never lose track of what your true goal is: self-reliance. Henry David Thoreau popularized the idea almost two hundred years ago and the concept worked its way so firmly into the fabric of American thinking that it has never once become obsolete or irrelevant.

While Thoreau connected self-reliance (in part) with the ability to grow all one's own food, I relate it to the ability to "grow" all one's own money. I promise you there is as much satisfaction in the planting as in the consumption.

# Glossary

account—Money deposited in a bank that may be withdrawn on demand by the depositor.

allowance—A specific amount of money the parent gives a child each week as a reward for being a working member of the family.

annual report—Formal financial statement issued by public companies each year.

automated teller machine (ATM)—A machine in a bank or at some other convenient place where people can withdraw or deposit money electronically.

bank—An institution where money may be safely kept and which lends money and provides other financial services.

bank statement—A record of deposits, withdrawals, fee charges, and interest earned on a particular account.

budget—A plan of how much money a person, business, government, or other organization has to spend and how it will be spent.

**canceled check**—A check that has been paid from an account and returned to the account holder.

**certificate of deposit (CD)**—A type of savings account where the money is deposited for an agreed amount of time.

**check**—A written order to a bank to pay a specified amount of money to a specific person or company from money on deposit with the bank.

**check register**—A log, book, or journal where each check is written in order.

**check stubs**—The portion of a check on which you may keep a record of the check.

**chore**—A routine task.

**collateral**—Property that a borrower promises to pay a lender in case of default on a loan.

**comparative value**—The price of one item as compared to another, similar item.

**consumer**—A person who buys goods or services for his own use.

**co-sign**—To sign a document for another person indicating responsibility to pay the amount owed if the borrower defaults on the loan.

**coupon**—A certificate entitling one to a discount when purchasing goods or services.

**credit**—Money loaned, usually for a fee, that must be paid back at a future time.

**credit card**—A card that allows people to make purchases on credit.

**credit report**—The record of a person's credit history that lending institutions use to determine whether or not that person is financially reliable.

**credit union**—A financial organization usually connected with a company or a professional association that offers some financial services to its members.

**currency**—Any kind of money that is used as a medium of exchange.

**custody**—The guardianship or safekeeping, usually of a child.

**debit**—To deduct money from your bank or other kind of account.

**debt**—The money you owe when you buy on credit or borrow from someone else.

**default**—To fail to pay back a loan.

**demand**—The desire and ability to pay for goods or services.

**denomination**—A category of bills or any other kind of money of particular value.

**deposit**—To place in a bank. Also, the sum of money that is put there.

**depression**—A period of serious recession marked by high unemployment and a decline in business and stock market values.

**dividends**—The profits that a company distributes to its stockholders.

**economy**—The structure of the flow of money in a society.

**Federal Reserve Bank**—Created in 1913 by Congress to stabilize the nation's economy, the Federal Reserve Bank is the central bank of the United States. It is divided into twelve regional banks that are spread across the country. The bank's main work is to control the supply of money. It holds a percentage of the funds (the reserves) of commercial banks and lends money to them when needed.

**environmental training**—As used in this book, it means the practical, hands-on knowledge you impart to your youngster as you go about your daily activities together.

**executor**—The person appointed to carry out the directions of a will.

**fee**—A fixed charge.

**finance**—The science of managing money.

**foreign exchange**—The value of one nation's currency in relation to another's.

**Fort Knox**—An army base in Kentucky where most of the United States's gold is stored.

**good(s)**—Anything of some value that may be traded for or bought.

**guardian**—A person legally in charge of the affairs of a minor.

**hedge against inflation**—An investment made now to protect a person or business from the risk of rising prices in the future.

**income**—Money received from labor or services, or from property, investments, etc.

**individual retirement account (IRA)**—A tax-deferred account used to save money for retirement.

**inflation**—An economic condition characterized by rising prices, usually caused by too much available money in the economy.

**inheritance**—Something, usually money, that is passed on to an individual after the death of another person.

**installment**—Partial payment of a debt.

**installment credit**—An arrangement between a store and a consumer that allows a purchase to be paid for in partial payments.

**insurance policy**—A contract guaranteeing financial protection in case of fire, accident, death, or other disaster.

**invest**—To risk money with hope of added financial return.

**Keogh account**—A tax-deferred retirement savings account for a person who is self-employed.

**lease**—A contract by which one party gives to another the use of land, buildings, property, and so forth for a specified time and for fixed payments.

**line of credit**—An agreed amount of money waiting at the bank that can be borrowed by a depositor.

**living expenses**—The total cost of basic necessities.

**loan**—A sum of money borrowed for a certain period of time, often involving interest paid to the lender by the borrower.

**maturity**—The end of a bond's interest-earning term or the last day when a loan is due.

**medium of exchange**—Anything that a group of people agree has a certain value.

**money**—Anything a group of people accept in exchange for goods or services.

**money market account**—A checking account that pays interest. It usually requires a minimum deposit and restricts the number of checks that can be written in a given time period.

**money order**—An order issued from a post office, bank, or other financial institution to pay a specified sum of money to a specified person or business.

**mortgage money**—Money loaned by a bank for the purpose of buying a house or other property.

**mutual fund**—A pooling of money by many people to be invested in stocks and bonds.

**odd job**—A chore or task not regularly done.

**offerings**—Money that is donated to a charity or charitable organization.

**passbook account**—A savings account in which the transactions are recorded in a book that must be given to the bank whenever a deposit or withdrawal is made.

**personal identification number (PIN)**—The secret number encoded onto a bank card that must be entered into the ATM machine before money can be withdrawn or deposited.

**portfolio**—A group of investments owned by a person.

**prime rate**—The interest rate that banks charge their largest and best customers.

**profit**—The money a business makes less the costs of producing and selling its products.

**recession**—A downturn in the economy, when the demand for goods declines and the money supply is less.

**register**—The section of a checkbook where you record your transactions.

**relative value**—The price of an item in relation to what it will cost the individual in work and time to earn the money necessary to buy the item.

**savings**—Money that is put somewhere safe so that it can be used later.

**service**—Any work that is done for money or barter.

**stock**—Shares of a company that may be purchased by the public.

**stock market**—The place where shares of many different companies are bought and sold.

**stockbroker**—A person who buys and sells stock on the stock market for other people.

**stockholder**—A person who owns stock (shares) in a company.

**supply**—The amount of something offered at a price for meeting demand.

**tax return**—A form that reviews the total annual earnings of an individual, married couple, or company in order to establish the amount of taxes due.

**trust fund**—Money or stock held in trust.

**unemployment rate**—The calculation of the percentage of people in a society who want to work but are unable to find jobs.

**value**—The worth of something as measured in goods, services, or a medium of exchange.

**will**—The legal statement of a person's wishes concerning the disposal of his property and care of his or her dependents after his or her death.

# Index